CAIRO TRAVEL GUIDE 2025

A Journey Through Ancient Pyramids, Vibrant Bazaars, and Modern Marvels

LIAM CASPIAN

WELCOME TO CAIRO EXPLORATION IN 2025

Copyright © 2025 by LIAM CASPIAN
All rights reserved.

Text, photos, and multimedia cannot be used without authorization from Liam Caspian, No part of this work may be reproduced, distributed, or without written authorization. To request authorization or licensing to reprint this composition, please communicate with Liam Caspian. Thank you. The brand notice shall serve as the defense to prove that all content is exclusive under U.S. and global brand laws.

We sincerely appreciate your support and hope you've enjoyed our travel guides. Taking a moment to leave a quick review would mean a lot to us and help others discover our products. Thank you for choosing our guides and for your ongoing encouragement!

TABLE OF CONTENTS
My Travel Memories

Introduction to Cairo: A Timeless City
- A Blend of Ancient and Modern
- Why Visit Cairo in 2025?

Chapter 1: History and Heritage: The Ancient Landmarks
- The Pyramids of Giza: A Wonder of the World
- The Sphinx: Guardian of the Sands
- Saqqara: The Step Pyramid and Ancient Necropolis
- The Egyptian Museum: Pharaohs, Mummies, and Antiquities

Chapter 2: The Heart of Cairo: Vibrant Markets and Bustling Streets
- Khan El Khalili: Shopping, Souvenirs, and Traditional Crafts
- Souq al-Gomaa: A Glimpse into Local Life
- Exploring the Streets of Islamic Cairo

Chapter 3: Cultural Experiences: Uncovering Cairo's Unique Charm
- The Citadel of Saladin: A Fortress of History
- Coptic Cairo: Churches and Ancient Christian Heritage

- Al-Azhar Mosque and University: A Center of Islamic Learning

Chapter 4: Contemporary Cairo: The Modern Spirit of the City
- Downtown Cairo: Modern Architecture and City Life
- New Cairo and Gated Communities: A Look at Cairo's Future
- Nile Cruises: From Traditional Feluccas to Luxury Vessels

Chapter 5: Dining in Cairo: Local Flavors and Global Cuisine
- Egyptian Cuisine: What to Try and Where to Eat
- Street Food in Cairo: Quick Bites and Flavorful Snacks
- Fine Dining and International Restaurants in the City

Chapter 6: Cairo by Night: Entertainment and Nightlife
- Rooftop Bars and Lounges with Nile Views
- Traditional Music and Dance: Experience Egyptian Folklore
- Cafés and Hookah Spots: Relax in Cairo's Evening Breeze

Chapter 7: Beyond the City: Day Trips and Excursions
- Alexandria: A Coastal Escape from Cairo
- The Fayoum Oasis: Nature and History Combined
- The Temples of Luxor: A Journey Through Time

Chapter 8: Staying in Cairo: Accommodation Options
- Luxury Hotels: Where History Meets Comfort
- Budget-Friendly Stays: Hostels and Guesthouses
- Boutique Hotels and Unique Lodging Experiences

Chapter 9: Practical Information and Travel Tips
- Best Times to Visit Cairo in 2025
- Transportation: Getting Around the City
- Essential Arabic Phrases for Travelers
- Health, Safety, and Local Etiquette

Chapter 10: Sustainability and Responsible Tourism in Cairo
- Eco-Friendly Accommodations
- Sustainable Dining: Where to Eat Responsibly
- Protecting Egypt's Historical Sites and Natural Environment

Chapter 11: Index
- Alphabetical Listing of Key Locations, Landmarks, and Topics

CONCLUSION

My Travel Memories

Cairo has always been celebrated for its enduring allure, where the ancient and the modern coexist in perfect harmony. Visiting Cairo in 2025 was an unforgettable journey through history, culture, and vibrant experiences, with every day revealing a new facet of this captivating city. Its lively streets pulse with activity, weaving a story that spans millennia while remaining vibrant and thoroughly modern.

Initial Encounter: Touching Down in Cairo

The moment I arrived in Cairo, I was met with an atmosphere that blended warmth with vibrant energy. The journey from Cairo International Airport to the city center unveiled a captivating skyline, where contemporary skyscrapers rose alongside historic districts. The city's vast expanse immediately caught my attention, sprawling endlessly in every direction, alive with the constant motion of people, vehicles, and daily life.

Cairo International Airport

Cairo's renowned traffic proved true to its reputation, but rather than being frustrating, it provided a glimpse into the city's unique rhythm. The constant honking of car horns felt like a language of its own, while street vendors navigated the bustling streets with ease, offering everything from tasty snacks to electronic gadgets.

Exploring the Ancient Wonders

No journey to Cairo is truly complete without exploring the Giza Plateau, where the iconic Pyramids and the Great Sphinx stand. Witnessing these legendary structures firsthand was an awe-inspiring experience that no photograph could ever fully convey. The immense scale of the pyramids took my breath away. Although I had read about them for years, standing at their base allowed me to truly appreciate their ancient engineering marvels. My guide, a local Egyptologist, enhanced the experience with captivating stories about the pyramid builders and the profound spiritual meaning behind these monumental feats.

Giza Plateau

Visiting the tomb of Pharaoh Khufu and admiring the Sphinx's imposing presence were moments that felt truly otherworldly. What made it even more remarkable was the feeling of timelessness. Despite the crowds of tourists, the site retained an enigmatic and majestic atmosphere that seemed to defy the passage of time.

Cairo's Bustling Markets and Street Life

After immersing myself in Cairo's ancient history, I ventured into the lively pulse of its modern streets. I spent an afternoon at Khan el-Khalili, one of the city's most historic markets, where narrow alleyways are lined with stalls offering everything from handcrafted jewelry to fragrant spices. The market is a vibrant labyrinth of sights and sounds, with vendors enthusiastically promoting their goods and the air thick with the scent of incense.

Khan el-Khalili

One of my standout moments was sitting at a traditional café, enjoying Egyptian mint tea, while observing the vibrant scene unfold around me. It was in that moment that I truly began to grasp Cairo's essence—where old-world traditions and contemporary life coexist in seamless harmony. The market was a sensory overload, yet each corner revealed something new, from artisans crafting detailed brass lamps to vendors offering colorful local fabrics.

Immersing in Cairo's Cultural Life

Cairo, beyond its historical significance, stands as a vibrant cultural center, and no trip would be complete without exploring its modern artistic offerings. One evening, I had the privilege of attending a performance at the Cairo Opera House, where I was captivated by a stunning fusion of classical music and traditional Egyptian dance. It was fascinating to witness how Egypt's rich heritage continues to shape its contemporary arts scene.

Another highlight of my visit was the Egyptian Museum, home to an extraordinary collection of ancient artifacts. The sheer size of the museum was awe-inspiring, particularly the Tutankhamun exhibit, where his iconic golden mask and other burial treasures are on display. As I wandered through the halls, the intricate artistry of ancient Egypt became even more striking, with each piece revealing a fragment of the country's remarkable past. What added a layer of significance to this experience was knowing that many of these exhibits will soon be moved to the Grand Egyptian Museum, a new cultural landmark set to open fully later in 2025.

Egyptian Museum

A Glimpse into Modern Cairo
Cairo's historic attractions are undeniably impressive, but the modern side of the city is equally captivating. I spent time exploring the neighborhoods of Zamalek and Garden City, two of Cairo's more upscale districts.

Zamalek, with its leafy streets and chic cafes, was a welcome break from the city's frenetic energy. Here, I indulged in a delicious meal at one of its many international restaurants, a reflection of Cairo's cosmopolitan nature.

I also took a boat ride along the Nile River, a peaceful contrast to the constant motion of the city. As the boat glided across the calm waters, the city's lights twinkled in the distance, offering a different perspective of Cairo's urban sprawl. This gentle cruise gave me a chance to reflect on the layers of history that lie beneath the surface of modern Cairo.

Culinary Discoveries

Cairo's food scene is a true sensory delight, offering everything from street eats to upscale dining. The variety of flavors and dishes is astounding, but I kept returning to classic Egyptian staples like koshari—a hearty combination of rice, lentils, and pasta topped with tangy tomato sauce—and falafel made from fava beans, a distinctive twist on the more common chickpea version. Street vendors often put their own unique spin on these recipes, making every bite feel like a new culinary adventure.

One evening, I visited a traditional restaurant in the heart of Islamic Cairo and tried molokhia, a richly flavored soup made from jute leaves, served with rice and chicken. Its earthy, slightly bitter taste was unlike anything I'd experienced before, showcasing how deeply Cairo's cuisine is rooted in tradition and heritage.

Day Trips Beyond Cairo

During my visit, I ventured beyond Cairo's bustling streets to explore the treasures outside the city. A short drive brought me to Saqqara, the site of Egypt's oldest pyramid—the Step Pyramid of Djoser. Unlike the busy Giza Plateau, Saqqara offered a more tranquil and personal glimpse into Egypt's ancient history. I also explored Memphis, the once-great capital of ancient Egypt, where I marveled at massive statues and the remains of grand temples that once symbolized the might of the Pharaohs.

Reflections on Cairo in 2025

Cairo in 2025 is a city of contrasts, firmly grounded in its rich history while swiftly moving toward the future. Here, you can marvel at ancient wonders in the morning, delve into a vibrant cultural scene in the afternoon, and admire a dazzling modern skyline by night. The city pulses with an energy that is at once captivating and intense, and it is within this dynamic blend of past and present that Cairo's unique charm truly shines.

Every moment of my journey deepened my admiration for Egypt's history, culture, and people. From the awe-inspiring majesty of the pyramids to the lively energy of downtown, Cairo is a city that invites endless discovery. More than that, it offers a profound connection to a rich and diverse past that continues to shape its vibrant daily life today.

Introduction to Cairo: A Timeless City

Cairo, Egypt's vast and vibrant capital, is a city that resists easy definition. Its streets carry the legacy of ancient pharaohs, medieval rulers, and contemporary life, creating a unique and multifaceted identity. Few cities in the world weave together such a profound historical heritage with the energy of the present. The result is a place that feels both timeless and ever-evolving—a remarkable blend where the ancient and modern exist in seamless harmony.

Cairo is more than a haven for history enthusiasts; it's a city that captivates in every sense. From the breathtaking silhouette of the Giza Pyramids to the vibrant hustle of the Khan el-Khalili bazaar, Cairo beckons exploration at every turn. It's a city where you can wander through narrow lanes infused with *the aroma of spices or stand in awe of the Nile as it gracefully courses through its heart. In Cairo, visitors are not mere spectators but active participants in a living story, uncovering the intricate layers of culture, heritage, and modernity that make this dynamic city truly unforgettable.*

A Blend of Ancient and Modern

At the heart of Cairo's charm lies its extraordinary fusion of the old and the new. This striking contrast is most evident in its skyline, where ancient pyramids stand side by side with sleek modern skyscrapers. The city boasts some of the world's most renowned landmarks, including the Pyramids of Giza, the Great Sphinx, and the priceless artifacts housed in the Egyptian Museum. Yet, amid these historical treasures, Cairo thrives as a contemporary metropolis, home to vibrant art galleries, upscale dining spots, bustling cafés, and dynamic neighborhoods like Zamalek and Maadi.

Strolling through Cairo is like stepping through different eras in a single day. You might start your morning exploring the ancient tombs of Giza and end it in a chic downtown café, sipping coffee as the sounds of modern city life surround you. This harmonious coexistence of the ancient and the contemporary is what makes Cairo truly captivating.

The city is not a relic of the past; it is ever-changing, with each generation adding new dimensions to its rich and complex identity.

The narrow lanes of Islamic Cairo, lined with intricate mosques and historic buildings, stand in stark contrast to the sprawling modern developments on the city's outskirts. One moment, you might marvel at the centuries-old artistry of Al-Azhar Mosque, and the next, you're immersed in modern Cairo at a trendy mall or cutting-edge gallery. It's this seamless blend of tradition and progress that makes Cairo endlessly fascinating, offering visitors a chance to experience both its timeless grandeur and vibrant present.

Al-Azhar Mosque

Why Visit Cairo in 2025?
Cairo in 2025 stands at the threshold of transformation, blending its storied past with an

exciting vision for the future. This year offers a unique opportunity to experience a city that continues to honor its rich heritage while embracing dynamic change. Whether your interests lie in history, culture, or modern urban development, 2025 is the perfect time to immerse yourself in Cairo's evolving narrative.

A key highlight of the year is the long-awaited opening of the Grand Egyptian Museum, a groundbreaking cultural venue located near the iconic Pyramids of Giza. This state-of-the-art museum will feature some of Egypt's most cherished treasures, including the full Tutankhamun collection, reimagined in a modern setting. While the Egyptian Museum in Tahrir Square remains an essential stop, the Grand Egyptian Museum introduces a new dimension to exploring Egypt's ancient legacy, pairing timeless artifacts with innovative exhibition design. Visiting Cairo in 2025 offers a rare chance to witness this milestone, marking a new chapter in the preservation and celebration of one of the world's greatest civilizations.

Grand Egyptian Museum

Cairo's cultural scene is also more vibrant than ever. From the flourishing local art movement to the city's increasingly sophisticated dining options, 2025 promises a deeper immersion into contemporary Egyptian life. The city's galleries are filled with works from both up-and-coming and established Egyptian artists, while the restaurant scene is embracing farm-to-table concepts and international culinary trends, alongside traditional Egyptian flavors. Whether you're sampling koshari from a street vendor or enjoying fine dining in a stylish restaurant overlooking the Nile, the food scene in Cairo offers a flavorful journey through the city's diverse influences.

Another reason to visit Cairo in 2025 is the growing focus on eco-conscious travel. The city is increasingly embracing sustainable tourism, with more eco-friendly accommodations and responsible travel initiatives popping up throughout the region. From hotels that prioritize water conservation and solar energy to tour operators who focus on reducing environmental impact, Cairo is becoming more aware of its role in global sustainability efforts. For visitors who are conscious of their ecological footprint, 2025 offers more opportunities to engage in responsible travel while still enjoying the richness of the city.

*Cairo's contemporary appeal is matched by its continued commitment to preserving its historical landmarks. Restoration projects are in full swing across the city, ensuring that visitors can experience the grandeur of sites like **Coptic Cairo**, the **Citadel**, and the **Mosque of Muhammad Ali** with renewed appreciation. These initiatives ensure that the timeless beauty of Cairo's heritage is maintained while adapting to the demands of the present day.*

Additionally, the hospitality scene in Cairo has evolved dramatically in recent years, offering visitors more choices than ever before. Whether you're looking for five-star luxury or a boutique guesthouse in a historic neighborhood, Cairo has accommodations to suit every traveler's taste. Hotels have embraced a blend of Egyptian tradition and modern comfort, with many incorporating local artistry, textiles, and crafts into their design, giving guests a deeper connection to the culture from the moment they arrive.

For travelers seeking more than just a typical tourist experience, Cairo in 2025 offers a variety of ways to connect with the local culture. From hands-on cooking classes and workshops with artisans to in-depth tours led by local historians, there are numerous opportunities to engage with the city on a personal level. This year's focus on cultural exchange has made Cairo an even more rewarding destination for travelers who want to delve beneath the surface.

In essence, Cairo in 2025 offers a rare chance to witness the convergence of ancient wonders and modern advancements. Whether you're standing before the Pyramids, marveling at the city's contemporary arts scene, or enjoying a meal overlooking the Nile, Cairo remains a city that captivates and surprises at every turn. Its timeless appeal is undeniable, yet in 2025, the city feels more relevant than ever—an essential destination for travelers who seek both the profound and the present.

Chapter One

History and Heritage: The Ancient Landmarks of Cairo

Cairo's ancient landmarks have stood for thousands of years, witnessing the rise and fall of empires, dynasties, and civilizations. The city's timeless history is etched into its monuments, offering visitors a chance to connect with some of the most iconic structures ever created. Whether you're drawn to the towering pyramids, the enigmatic Sphinx, the ancient necropolis of Saqqara, or the treasures housed in the

Egyptian Museum, Cairo's heritage is a remarkable journey into the distant past. Here's a deeper look at these monumental sites and their significance

The Pyramids of Giza: A Wonder of the World

The Pyramids of Giza are one of the most enduring symbols of ancient Egypt and a testament to the ingenuity of its people. Built over 4,500 years ago, these pyramids continue to captivate the world with their immense size and architectural precision. The Great Pyramid, built for Pharaoh Khufu, was the tallest man-made structure in the world for centuries. Standing at 146 meters (481 feet), it remains an awe-inspiring sight. The precision of the blocks, the scale of the construction, and the alignment with the stars all add to the mystery and intrigue surrounding these ancient tombs.

Beyond the sheer size, the pyramids represent the ancient Egyptians' deep beliefs in the afterlife. These monumental structures were designed as eternal resting places for the pharaohs, filled with everything they might need in the next world. Today, walking around the Pyramids of Giza offers a glimpse into the power and grandeur of Egypt's Old Kingdom.

The Sphinx: Guardian of the Sands

Lying close to the pyramids is the Great Sphinx of Giza, another iconic symbol of Egypt's ancient history. Carved from a single piece of limestone, the Sphinx has the body of a lion and the head of a human—believed to represent Pharaoh Khafre. At 73 meters (240 feet) long and 20 meters (66 feet) high, it stands as a guardian of the necropolis, its gaze fixed eternally toward the rising sun.

Despite the erosion of time, the Sphinx retains its mystique. Its origins are shrouded in legend, with scholars still debating its exact purpose and the meaning behind its enigmatic expression. Visitors to the Sphinx are often struck by its scale and the atmosphere of reverence that surrounds it. As the desert winds swirl around this timeless figure, it's easy to see why it has inspired wonder for generations.

Saqqara: The Step Pyramid and Ancient Necropolis

While the Pyramids of Giza are world-famous, the ancient site of Saqqara offers a different perspective on Egypt's architectural evolution. Located a short distance from Cairo, Saqqara is home to the **Step**

Pyramid of Djoser, the first pyramid ever built. This structure, designed by the brilliant architect Imhotep, marked the transition from simple mastaba tombs to the complex pyramid structures that would follow. Its six-tiered design was revolutionary in its time, standing at 60 meters (197 feet).

Saqqara is more than just the Step Pyramid; it is an expansive necropolis that served as the burial ground for Memphis, Egypt's ancient capital. The site is filled with tombs, temples, and smaller pyramids, offering insights into the burial practices and beliefs of early Egyptian civilization. The tombs of nobles and officials are decorated with vivid murals and inscriptions, depicting scenes of daily life and religious ceremonies. Saqqara is a quieter, less

crowded alternative to Giza, where visitors can explore Egypt's ancient past at a more relaxed pace.

The Egyptian Museum: Pharaohs, Mummies, and Antiquities

Cairo's **Egyptian Museum** is a treasure trove of history, housing one of the world's largest collections of ancient Egyptian artifacts. Located in Tahrir Square, this museum offers visitors a chance to see thousands of objects that span over 5,000 years of Egypt's history. The most famous of these is the collection from the tomb of **Tutankhamun**, including the pharaoh's iconic gold mask. Discovered in the Valley of the Kings in 1922, Tutankhamun's burial treasures are some of the most exquisite examples of ancient Egyptian craftsmanship.

Another highlight of the museum is the **Mummy Room**, where visitors can see the preserved bodies of some of Egypt's most famous rulers, including **Ramses II**. The intricate process of mummification, perfected over millennia, allowed the ancient Egyptians to preserve their dead in remarkable detail. These mummies, encased in elaborately decorated coffins, provide a tangible link to Egypt's ancient rulers and their quest for immortality.

The Egyptian Museum's collection goes far beyond pharaohs and mummies. It includes statues, jewelry, papyrus scrolls, and everyday objects from ancient Egypt. Each artifact tells a story, whether of royal grandeur or the daily lives of ordinary Egyptians. As Cairo looks forward to the opening of the **Grand Egyptian Museum,** *the Egyptian Museum remains a must-visit for anyone interested in exploring Egypt's unparalleled historical legacy.*

Cairo's ancient landmarks are not just remnants of a distant past—they are living connections to one of the most influential civilizations in human history. The Pyramids of Giza, the Sphinx, Saqqara, and the Egyptian Museum each offer a unique window into the beliefs, achievements, and mysteries of the ancient world. These landmarks invite visitors to step back in time and experience the grandeur, spirituality, and ingenuity that have made Egypt a cornerstone of global heritage. Whether it's the towering pyramids or the treasures of Tutankhamun, Cairo's history will leave an indelible mark on anyone who walks in its footsteps.

Chapter Two

The Heart of Cairo: Vibrant Markets and Bustling Streets

In the heart of Cairo, where the ancient and modern converge, there's an energy that fills every corner. The markets and streets of Cairo are not just places to shop; they are experiences that immerse visitors in the city's rich cultural fabric. The sights, sounds, and smells are part of the adventure, with the hum of everyday life creating a captivating rhythm. Whether you're navigating the historic alleys of **Khan El Khalili**, diving into the authenticity of **Souq al-Gomaa**, or wandering the narrow lanes of **Islamic Cairo**, each market tells a story and offers an *unforgettable glimpse into this dynamic city. Here's what makes these areas truly special.*

Khan El Khalili: Shopping, Souvenirs, and Traditional Crafts

No visit to Cairo is complete without stepping into **Khan El Khalili,** *one of the city's oldest and most famous markets. Dating back to the 14th century, Khan El Khalili has evolved into a bustling labyrinth of alleyways, where traders sell everything from hand-crafted silver jewelry to intricately woven carpets, brassware, and vibrant fabrics. The market is a sensory feast—gold glitters in shop windows, the smell of spices fills the air, and the sound of merchants haggling with customers creates an atmosphere alive with tradition.*

For centuries, the market has been a hub of craftsmanship. Artisans continue to produce items using techniques passed down through generations, ensuring that the objects you find here are more than just souvenirs—they are pieces of Cairo's living heritage. Whether it's a delicate filigree necklace or an ornate shisha pipe, each item has a story rooted in the city's artistic soul.

One of the market's undeniable charms is the opportunity to watch the craftsmen at work. Stroll through the winding streets, and you might catch sight of a silversmith hammering out a new design, a potter shaping clay into traditional vessels, or a weaver spinning colorful threads into fabric. Khan El

Khalili is a place where the past and present coexist, and every turn reveals something new to discover.

Souq al-Gomaa: A Glimpse into Local Life

*For a more off-the-beaten-path experience, head to **Souq al-Gomaa**, the bustling Friday market that offers an authentic slice of Egyptian life. Located near the City of the Dead, this sprawling bazaar is as much about the locals as it is about the goods for sale. Unlike the more tourist-focused Khan El Khalili, Souq al-Gomaa gives visitors a window into how Cairenes barter, haggle, and trade.*

The market is a treasure trove of eclectic finds. Here, you'll see everything from second-hand clothes and

household items to antiques and unique curiosities. It's a place where one person's unwanted object becomes another's prized possession, and the atmosphere is electric with the exchange of goods and stories.

Navigating Souq al-Gomaa requires a bit of patience and a sense of adventure, but the rewards are plentiful for those willing to explore. This market, with its colorful chaos, embodies the vibrancy of local Cairo. It is less polished than the more tourist-centric markets, but that's precisely its charm. If you're seeking a more authentic encounter with Cairo's street life, this market will give you exactly that—an unfiltered experience where you're shoulder-to-shoulder with the city's residents.

Exploring the Streets of Islamic Cairo

Islamic Cairo is a historical treasure, and its streets are a living museum. This area is home to some of the city's most important Islamic monuments and mosques, but beyond its architectural beauty, the narrow alleyways buzz with daily life. As you meander through the streets, you'll encounter a blend of history and commerce, where medieval buildings house modern shops and bustling workshops.

*Start your exploration at **Al-Muizz Street**, a main artery running through Islamic Cairo, where centuries-old mosques and madrasas line the way. The street offers a fascinating journey through time, with the **Al-Azhar Mosque** and **Sultan Hassan Mosque** standing as testaments to the city's religious and cultural significance. Their towering minarets dominate the skyline, while the intricate tilework and carvings on the buildings reflect the incredible craftsmanship of past eras.*

*But the charm of Islamic Cairo isn't limited to its historical monuments. Its streets are alive with vendors selling traditional sweets, fresh bread, and spices. Here, you can experience the local flavors of Egypt, whether you're sampling a warm (Egyptian pastry) from a street vendor or buying fragrant **hibiscus tea** to take home. The lively atmosphere, paired with the timeless architecture, makes every step an invitation to engage with Cairo's layered history.*

As you wander deeper into the streets, you'll discover hidden treasures at every corner—traditional perfumeries selling essential oils, old bookstores filled with rare Arabic texts, and workshops where artisans craft everything from wooden inlay boxes to delicate copper lanterns. The spirit of Islamic Cairo is tangible in these moments, as you step into spaces that have remained largely unchanged for generations.

Cairo's vibrant markets and streets provide an authentic pulse of the city. Khan El Khalili showcases the artistic legacy of Egypt, where centuries of craftsmanship meet modern demands. Souq al-Gomaa offers a more grounded experience, a chaotic yet captivating look at daily life, while Islamic Cairo invites visitors to walk through history, where ancient monuments coexist with thriving markets. These areas are not just places to buy souvenirs—they are windows into Cairo's soul. Each market, each street, tells a story, and exploring them brings you closer to the heart of this remarkable city.

Chapter Three

Cultural Experiences: Uncovering Cairo's Unique Charm

Cairo, one of the world's most historic cities, offers an unparalleled journey through time. Its unique blend of ancient legacies and modern culture creates an atmosphere where every corner reveals a story. From its towering fortresses to sacred spaces that have shaped spiritual and academic thought for centuries, Cairo is a living museum. This ancient metropolis invites visitors to delve deep into its heart and witness how its remarkable cultural landmarks continue to shape its identity today.

The Citadel of Saladin: A Fortress of History

Dominating the skyline from the elevated Mokattam Hills, the **Citadel of Saladin** is one of Cairo's most significant and awe-inspiring landmarks. Built in the late 12th century by the legendary Muslim leader Saladin, it was constructed as a defense against Crusader forces and served as the seat of Egyptian rulers for nearly 700 years. With its strategic location overlooking the city, the Citadel was more than just a military fortification—it was a symbol of power and authority for successive dynasties, from the Ayyubids to the Ottomans and beyond.

Citadel of Saladin

*Visitors to the Citadel are immediately struck by its vastness, with its walls enclosing a series of palaces, mosques, and museums. One of its most iconic structures is the **Mosque of Muhammad Ali** also known as the Alabaster Mosque. Built in the 19th century, this impressive structure, with its prominent domes and minarets, stands as a testament to Ottoman architectural influence. The mosque's ornate interior, with its stunning chandeliers and elegant calligraphy, offers a moment of reflection within the bustling energy of the city below.*

Mosque of Muhammad Ali

*Exploring the Citadel also means discovering the **Gawhara Palace**, the former residence of Muhammad Ali, and the **National Military Museum**, which offers a* *fascinating overview of Egypt's military history. From ancient pharaonic warfare to modern military advancements, the museum provides insight into the strategic importance of the Citadel throughout history.*

What makes the Citadel truly special is the sense of stepping into Cairo's past while enjoying panoramic views of its modern skyline. From the highest points of the fortress, visitors can see the city stretching endlessly below—a visual reminder of how Cairo has evolved, yet remains deeply rooted in its rich history.

Coptic Cairo: Churches and Ancient Christian Heritage

Coptic Cairo

*Nestled within the vibrant fabric of Cairo lies **Coptic Cairo**, a district where Egypt's Christian heritage is preserved in its quiet churches and religious sites. This neighborhood holds deep significance for Egypt's Coptic Orthodox community and is a testament to the country's religious diversity and long-standing Christian traditions that predate the Arab conquest.*

*One of the most renowned sites in Coptic Cairo is the **Hanging Church** (Saint Virgin Mary's Coptic Orthodox Church), so named because it was built atop the gates of the Roman Fortress of Babylon. With its wooden roof designed to resemble Noah's Ark, and a beautiful series of icons and mosaics, the Hanging Church is one of the oldest and most revered Christian structures in Egypt. Its serene atmosphere offers visitors a place of reflection and a glimpse into the early Christian community that thrived here.*

*Another important site is the **Church of St. Sergius and Bacchus**, a key pilgrimage destination for its association with the Holy Family's journey through Egypt. According to tradition, the church was built over a cave where Mary, Joseph, and the infant Jesus sought refuge during their flight from King Herod. The simple, yet profound, beauty of the church invites visitors to reflect on the deeply rooted Christian history that has shaped this region for millennia.*

*The **Coptic Museum** further enriches the experience, showcasing a remarkable collection of artifacts that detail the history of Christianity in Egypt. From ancient manuscripts to stunning textiles and stone carvings, the museum offers a fascinating window into the life, art, and beliefs of Egypt's early Christians.*

Coptic Cairo is not just a historical district; it is a vibrant part of the city where ancient faith meets modern life. The religious harmony in this area is a profound reminder of Cairo's multi-faith heritage, where churches and mosques exist side by side, weaving together a complex spiritual tapestry that defines the city's cultural fabric.

Al-Azhar Mosque and University: A Center of Islamic Learning

A place where faith, education, and history intersect, **Al-Azhar Mosque and University** stands as one of Cairo's most influential cultural and religious institutions. Established in 970 AD by the Fatimid Caliphate, Al-Azhar is one of the world's oldest universities, renowned for its role in shaping Islamic thought and theology over the centuries.

Al-Azhar Mosque

As a mosque, Al-Azhar is a magnificent example of Islamic architecture, with its elegant minarets and spacious marble courtyards. The mosque serves as a place of worship for Muslims, but it is also a center of intellectual and spiritual exchange, where discussions on Islamic jurisprudence, philosophy, and science *have taken place for over a thousand years. Stepping into Al-Azhar, one is immediately struck by its atmosphere of contemplation and learning, as students and scholars gather to read and discuss ancient texts.*

The university, which grew from the mosque, has long been a hub of Islamic scholarship. It attracts students from all over the world, drawn to its reputation as a place where Islamic tradition and modern thought come together. Al-Azhar's contributions to global Islamic learning are immeasurable; it has fostered dialogue between different schools of Islamic thought and continues to play a key role in religious and political discourse across the Muslim world.

Al-Azhar University gate

Visitors to Al-Azhar can explore its mosque, soaking in its peaceful ambiance while observing the legacy of learning that continues to thrive here. Its importance extends beyond Cairo, influencing scholars and religious leaders worldwide.

The cultural landmarks of Cairo—whether in the monumental strength of the **Citadel of Saladin,** the spiritual haven of **Coptic Cairo,** or the intellectual and religious beacon of **Al-Azhar Mosque and University** —capture the essence of a city where history and culture are inseparable. These are not mere attractions; they are living parts of Cairo's story, reflecting its role as a crossroads of civilizations, faiths, and ideas. As visitors walk through these spaces, they connect with centuries of human endeavor, creativity, and resilience—experiences that remain as vibrant and relevant today as they were in ancient times.

Chapter Four
Contemporary Cairo: The Modern Spirit of the City

Downtown Cairo: Modern Architecture and City Life in 2025

Downtown Cairo is a captivating blend of past and present, where modernity meets the city's historical layers. As the pulse of Egypt's capital, this district is a reflection of Cairo's transformation over the decades, offering a dynamic contrast to its ancient landmarks. In 2025, downtown Cairo continues to evolve, with its streets filled with energy, commerce, and culture. It's a place where sleek modern buildings stand alongside colonial architecture, and where the daily rhythm of life reveals the true spirit of this thriving metropolis.

A Journey Through Time: From Colonial to Contemporary

Originally designed in the 19th century under the vision of Egypt's ruler, Khedive Ismail, downtown Cairo was meant to mimic the grand boulevards of Paris. Wide streets, open squares, and European-style architecture defined the area, marking a significant departure from the winding alleys and traditional structures found in Islamic Cairo. Walking through this part of the city, visitors are still able to see the influence of that era, from the majestic façades of old cinemas and hotels to the elegant mansions that speak of a bygone time.

Today, these architectural remnants coexist with the sharp lines of glass-fronted office buildings, luxury apartments, and trendy cafes that cater to a new generation of urban dwellers. One of the most prominent landmarks in this part of the city is **Tahrir Square**, not only known for its political importance but also for the way it encapsulates the city's modern spirit. The square has been revitalized in recent years, with green spaces and clean, open areas providing a contrast to its historic role as the heart of Cairo's many revolutions.

Modern Cairo: Life on the Move

2025 finds downtown Cairo bustling with life and movement. The streets are filled with a mix of locals and tourists, government officials and entrepreneurs, artists and students. This is a district where global trends and traditional Egyptian life intersect seamlessly. The fashionable young crowds sipping coffee in hip cafes rub shoulders with vendors selling everything from books to homemade crafts, creating a unique tapestry of city life that can only be found in Cairo.

The **Cairo Metro**, Egypt's modern underground transport system, is one of the main arteries that keep downtown connected to the rest of the sprawling city. Convenient, efficient, and constantly expanding, it plays a key role in the daily commute for many residents. Navigating through the area's major stations like Sadat or Attaba, you'll find yourself amidst a constant stream of life, from busy professionals to street performers offering a brief cultural interlude in this fast-paced environment.

Shopping is another central part of the downtown experience, and visitors will find a mix of local boutiques, high-end brands, and traditional markets in the area. Stores along streets like Talaat Harb or Abdel Khalek Sarwat showcase the variety that modern Cairo has to offer—whether it's fashion, electronics, or books, downtown is a retail hub where you can spend hours exploring its labyrinth of shops.

The New Face of Downtown: Revitalization and Innovation

One of the most exciting developments in downtown Cairo in 2025 is the ongoing revitalization of the area. As the Egyptian government and private developers seek to preserve the historic character of the district while accommodating modern needs, new projects are popping up that balance innovation with tradition. Many of the historic buildings have been restored, transforming once-neglected spaces into vibrant cultural hubs, modern offices, and boutique hotels.

The new **Grand Egyptian Museum**, though technically located near the Giza Pyramids, has had an impact on downtown as well. Many visitors stay in downtown hotels and explore the museum's incredible collection of artifacts as part of their experience in Cairo, creating a new flow of tourism through the city's core.

Meanwhile, art galleries and performance spaces have been multiplying in the area, showcasing the work of contemporary Egyptian artists and performers. Venues such as **Cairo Opera House** and **Townhouse Gallery** contribute to the city's flourishing creative scene, providing both residents and visitors with an opportunity to engage with Egypt's modern cultural identity. These spaces blend seamlessly with the urban environment, offering a stark contrast to the more traditional parts of Cairo, and yet they fit naturally within the city's ever-evolving narrative.

Cairo Opera House

<u>*Nightlife and Dining: The Flavor of Downtown*</u>
When the sun sets, downtown Cairo comes alive in a completely different way. The streets, which are already crowded during the day, take on a new energy at night. Cafes and restaurants remain open late into the evening, and the city's residents embrace the cooler hours with leisurely strolls, impromptu gatherings, and late-night meals. The cuisine of downtown Cairo reflects the diversity of the city itself. From humble street food stalls serving up classics like koshari and falafel to high-end restaurants offering gourmet takes on

Egyptian and international dishes, the culinary scene is as varied as it is flavorful.

In recent years, a growing number of rooftop bars and lounges have become popular in downtown, offering stunning views of the city's skyline. Places like the **Cairo Capital Club** and **Zööba** have become favorites among both locals and tourists, offering a relaxing atmosphere with sweeping views of the Nile River or the bustling streets below. For those looking to experience Cairo's social scene, these rooftops are the perfect place to unwind after a day of exploration.

Downtown Cairo in 2025 is a vibrant and constantly shifting district that reflects the city's past, present, and future. It's a place where history, culture, and modern life intersect in unexpected and exciting ways. From its grand colonial buildings to its sleek new structures, from traditional markets to cutting-edge galleries, this part of the city is a living embodiment of Cairo's ability to adapt and grow while maintaining its unique character.

For travelers, a visit to downtown Cairo offers more than just sightseeing—it's a chance to immerse oneself in the daily life of Egypt's capital, to experience the city's pulse, and to witness firsthand how one of the world's most historic cities continues to evolve with the times. Whether you're wandering through its busy streets, admiring its architecture, or enjoying a meal in one of its lively restaurants, downtown Cairo offers an unforgettable experience that is both deeply rooted in history and firmly connected to the future.

New Cairo and Gated Communities: A Look at Cairo's Future

As Cairo continues to expand and modernize, New Cairo has emerged as a symbol of the city's future. Located on the outskirts of the capital, this sprawling area was conceived as a solution to

Cairo's urban congestion and offers a glimpse into the rapidly changing landscape of Egyptian city life. With wide avenues, modern infrastructure, and a carefully planned layout, New Cairo represents a stark contrast to the dense, chaotic streets of the old city. It has quickly become a desirable location for the city's growing middle and upper classes, as well as for international businesses and institutions seeking a foothold in Egypt.

The Birth of New Cairo: Planning for a Growing Population

In the late 1990s, the Egyptian government launched an ambitious plan to ease the pressure on Cairo's overstretched resources by developing a series of satellite cities. New Cairo, one of the largest and most successful of these projects, was envisioned as a modern urban center that would attract residents and businesses away from the overcrowded downtown areas. Spanning over 70,000 acres, New Cairo's development was designed with long-term sustainability in mind, featuring green spaces, wide roads, and designated residential, commercial, and educational zones.

Today, New Cairo stands as a prime example of what a planned urban area in Egypt can achieve. Its spacious layout, clean environment, and relative tranquility have made it a popular choice for those looking to escape the hustle and bustle of traditional Cairo. The population of New Cairo is growing rapidly, with many of Cairo's elite, professionals, and expatriates making the move to this suburban haven.

Gated Communities: A New Way of Life
One of the most defining features of New Cairo is its abundance of **gated communities**, which have become synonymous with the area's upscale lifestyle. These communities offer a level of privacy, security, and exclusivity that is highly sought after by Cairo's affluent residents. Behind the walls of these developments lie meticulously landscaped grounds, luxurious villas, modern apartments, and a wide array of amenities that cater to the needs of their inhabitants.

Gated communities like **Al Rehab**, **Mivida**, and **Katameya Heights** are some of the most well-known and desirable in New Cairo. These self-contained neighborhoods are equipped with schools, hospitals, shopping centers, sports clubs, and even entertainment facilities, offering residents a complete lifestyle within the community's boundaries. For many, living in these gated enclaves represents not just a move toward modernity, but a shift in how city dwellers interact with their environment, prioritizing space, comfort, and convenience.

Al Rehab, one of the first and most established of New Cairo's gated communities, is often viewed as a city within a city. Its design emphasizes walkability, with homes and apartments located close to amenities like parks, cafes, and retail outlets. Similarly, **Mivida** and **Katameya Heights** cater to luxury seekers, with elegant villas, golf courses, and world-class facilities that reflect a level of opulence previously unseen in Egypt's residential areas.

Al Rehab

A Hub for Education, Business, and Innovation

Beyond its residential appeal, New Cairo is also becoming a major hub for education and business. Several prestigious international schools and universities, such as the **American University in Cairo (AUC),** have established campuses in the area, attracting both local and international students. These institutions play a crucial role in fostering the next generation of Egyptian leaders and innovators, while also drawing attention from global companies and investors.

American University in Cairo (AUC)

Business is booming in New Cairo as well. With its modern infrastructure and ample space for development, the area has attracted many multinational corporations, tech startups, and regional headquarters. The rise of office parks and business districts in the area has helped position New Cairo as one of the most important economic zones in Egypt. This, in turn, has boosted the area's real estate market, with more people moving to New Cairo for work and seeking the live-work balance that this modern part of the city offers.

The Future of Urban Living in Cairo

New Cairo is not only a response to the overcrowded nature of traditional Cairo; it is also a model for what urban living in Egypt could look like in the future. As the city continues to grow, the demand for cleaner, more organized, and sustainable living spaces is on the rise. The concept of suburban expansion through developments like New Cairo is likely to continue, with further satellite cities and gated communities planned across the country.

In 2025, New Cairo is more than just a place to live; it's a symbol of progress and a reflection of Egypt's efforts to embrace modernization while maintaining its unique identity. As more people flock to the area, the need for efficient transportation systems, environmental sustainability, and infrastructure development becomes even more pressing. Fortunately, ongoing investments and innovations suggest that New Cairo will continue to evolve, becoming an even more desirable place to live, work, and raise families in the years to come.

New Cairo represents a significant shift in how urban life is being reimagined in Egypt. Its expensive gated communities, high-end amenities, and thoughtful urban planning provide a striking contrast to the historic and often hectic streets of central Cairo. As the area continues to grow and attract new residents, businesses, and educational institutions, it is becoming clear that New Cairo is not just a temporary solution to urban overcrowding but a lasting cornerstone of Egypt's urban future.

For those visiting Cairo or planning to relocate, New Cairo offers a glimpse of the country's aspirations toward a modern, livable city, where comfort and convenience are blended with forward-thinking design. While the area may lack the ancient landmarks that define other parts of Cairo, it is undoubtedly shaping the future of life in Egypt's capital, offering a new perspective on what it means to live in one of the world's most storied cities.

Nile Cruises: From Traditional Feluccas to Luxury Vessels

Cairo's iconic Nile River has been the lifeblood of Egypt for millennia, and today it continues to offer visitors a unique way to experience the country's landscapes and history. Nile cruises offer a journey through time, blending ancient wonders with the comfort and style of modern travel. Whether aboard a traditional felucca or a luxurious cruise ship, a journey down the Nile is an unforgettable experience that immerses travelers in the heart of Egypt's past and present.

Traditional Feluccas: Timeless Simplicity on the Nile

The **felucca**, a small wooden sailing boat, has been a fixture on the Nile for thousands of years. These wind-powered vessels, with their distinctive triangular sails, offer a simple yet authentic way to explore the river. Unlike modern cruise ships, feluccas operate without engines, relying solely on the wind to guide their gentle journey across the water. This peaceful, eco-friendly mode of transport provides an intimate and tranquil way to experience the Nile.

Aboard a felucca, time seems to slow down. The rhythmic flapping of the sails and the soft splashing of the water against the hull create a meditative atmosphere. Travelers can relax, lying on the cushioned deck, as the boat meanders past palm-fringed riverbanks, traditional villages, and ancient monuments. Sailing on a felucca offers a unique perspective on Egypt, allowing visitors to experience the country much as its people have for centuries—through the gentle rhythm of the Nile.

Felucca rides, often lasting a few hours or a day, are popular with both tourists and locals. In Cairo, many felucca operators offer short trips that provide stunning views of the city's skyline, especially at sunset, when the light softens and reflects off the river's surface. For those looking for a longer, more immersive experience, felucca tours can also be arranged to explore other sections of the Nile, providing an up-close view of the serene Egyptian countryside.

Luxury Nile Cruises: Modern Comfort Meets Ancient History
For those seeking a more indulgent experience, **luxury Nile cruises** provide an elegant and comfortable way to explore the river's storied

shores. These vessels, often resembling floating five-star hotels, offer all the amenities of modern travel while still allowing passengers to take in the wonders of Egypt from the water. Luxury cruises range from shorter two- or three-day journeys to longer week-long adventures that travel between Cairo, Luxor, and Aswan, stopping at iconic sites along the way.

Onboard a luxury Nile cruise, guests can expect spacious cabins, gourmet dining, and a range of entertainment and leisure activities, from sunbathing on the deck to enjoying nightly performances of traditional Egyptian music and dance. Many luxury ships are equipped with swimming pools, spas, and even fitness centers, ensuring that travelers are pampered throughout their journey. However, the true highlight of any Nile cruise is the opportunity to visit some of Egypt's most famous landmarks, all while traveling in style.

Popular cruise itineraries typically include visits to the ancient temples of **Karnak** and **Luxor**, the **Valley of the Kings**, and the stunning temple of **Abu Simbel** in the south. Guides accompany passengers onshore excursions, offering detailed insights into Egypt's rich history and helping to bring these extraordinary sites to life. The combination of history, luxury, and the scenic beauty of the Nile makes these cruises a favored choice for travelers looking to explore Egypt at a leisurely pace.

Choosing Your Nile Cruise Experience

Choosing between a traditional felucca and a luxury cruise depends on what kind of experience travelers are seeking. For those who wish to feel a deeper connection to Egypt's ancient traditions and appreciate a slower pace, the simple elegance of a felucca may be the perfect choice. The intimate setting, the absence of modern distractions, and the ability to glide quietly along the Nile's waters evoke the timelessness of the river itself.

On the other hand, luxury cruises cater to travelers looking for comfort, convenience, and a more structured itinerary. These vessels provide an all-inclusive experience, ensuring that guests can relax while visiting some of Egypt's most renowned archaeological sites. Whether enjoying a meal with panoramic river views or lounging on the sun deck with a cocktail, a luxury cruise offers a serene yet indulgent way to explore Egypt's ancient wonders.

Combining Tradition and Luxury: Dahabiya Cruises

For those seeking a blend of tradition and luxury, the **dahabiya** offers a middle ground. These traditional Egyptian sailboats are larger than feluccas but smaller than modern cruise ships, often accommodating only a handful of passengers. Dahabiya cruises offer an intimate, personalized experience with all the comforts of a luxury vessel, including private cabins, gourmet meals, and attentive service.

Dahabiyas are wind-powered like feluccas, but unlike their smaller counterparts, they come equipped with modern amenities and offer multi-day excursions that rival those of larger ships. Sailing aboard a dahabiya allows for a more leisurely and immersive exploration of the Nile, as the smaller size of these vessels permits access to less-visited sites that larger cruise ships cannot reach. This makes for a more private and exclusive experience, all while maintaining the charm of traditional Nile sailing.

The Nile: A Journey Through Time

Regardless of the vessel you choose, a Nile cruise is a journey through the heart of Egypt's past and present. As you sail the world's longest river, the landscapes shift from the modern cityscape of Cairo to ancient temples, lush farmlands, and timeless villages. The Nile's enduring presence throughout Egypt's history adds a layer of depth to the experience, as travelers find themselves following in the wake of the pharaohs, explorers, and traders who once navigated these same waters.

In 2025, Nile cruises continue to be one of the most memorable ways to discover Egypt's rich heritage. Whether it's the quiet simplicity of a felucca or the refined luxury of a cruise ship, the Nile offers an ever-changing panorama of natural beauty, ancient history, and vibrant culture, making it an essential part of any visit to this captivating country.

Chapter Five

Dining in Cairo: Local Flavors and Global Cuisine

Egyptian Cuisine: What to Try and Where to Eat

Exploring Egypt wouldn't be complete without immersing yourself in its rich culinary traditions. Egyptian cuisine is a reflection of the country's diverse cultural history, blending flavors from the Middle East, North Africa, and the Mediterranean. From hearty street food to elegant dining, every dish tells a story of Egypt's past and present. In Cairo, the vibrant food scene offers something for every taste, from traditional meals that have been prepared the same way for centuries to modern interpretations by contemporary chefs. Here's a guide to the must-try dishes and where to experience them during your visit.

Must-Try Egyptian Dishes
1.Koshari

Koshari is often considered Egypt's national dish. A true street food classic, this hearty meal is a delicious mix of rice, lentils, pasta, and chickpeas topped with tomato sauce, garlic vinegar, and crispy fried onions. It's a perfect balance of textures and flavors, offering both comfort and satisfaction. Simple yet filling, koshari is a vegetarian-friendly dish that you'll find in street stalls and casual eateries across the country.

Where to try it: Head to ***Koshary Abou Tarek*** in downtown Cairo for one of the city's best renditions of this beloved dish. The restaurant is famous among locals and visitors alike for its quick service and authentic flavors.

2.*Ful Medames*

Ful is a traditional Egyptian breakfast staple made from slow-cooked fava beans seasoned with olive oil, garlic, and lemon juice. Served with bread, it's often accompanied by fresh vegetables, boiled eggs, or even a drizzle of tahini. A simple yet nutritious dish, ful is a popular street food and also a breakfast favorite in Egyptian homes.

Where to try it: For a local experience, visit *Felfela*, a long-standing restaurant known for its classic Egyptian dishes. Here, you can enjoy a hearty breakfast of ful alongside other Egyptian specialties in a cozy, traditional setting.

3.*Taameya (Egyptian Falafel)*

Taameya, the Egyptian version of falafel, is a must-try for anyone visiting the country. Made from fava beans rather than chickpeas, as in other regions, Egyptian is typically flavored with fresh herbs and spices, giving it a green, vibrant interior. Crispy on the outside and soft on the inside, is often served in pita bread with tahini, salad, and pickles.

Where to try it: *El Tahrir* is one of Cairo's most famous falafel chains, serving up freshly fried that locals swear by. Their simple menu and no-frills approach have earned them a loyal following.

4.*Molokhia*

A dish with roots that go back to ancient Egypt, molokhia is a green soup made from finely chopped jute leaves simmered in broth with garlic and coriander. Its slightly gelatinous texture and earthy flavor make it a unique addition to Egyptian cuisine. Molokhia is often served with rice or bread, and sometimes paired with chicken or rabbit.

Where to try it: For a traditional molokhia experience, visit *El Dar Darak* in the Khan El Khalili district. This cozy eatery specializes in home-cooked Egyptian dishes and serves molokhia just like it's made in Egyptian households.

5.*Fattah*

A celebratory dish often prepared for special occasions, fattah is a layered dish made with rice, crispy bread, and slow-cooked meat, all topped with a rich tomato sauce and garlic vinegar. While it's commonly served during religious feasts, fattah can also be found in restaurants throughout the year. Its robust flavors make it a memorable meal that highlights Egypt's love for bold seasoning.

Where to try it: *Kebdet El Prince* in Imbaba is a great place to try fattah. This restaurant is a favorite among locals for its hearty portions and authentic Egyptian flavors.

6.Hawawshi

For those who love savory stuffed bread, is a must-try. It's made from pita bread stuffed with spiced ground meat, onions, and peppers, then baked or grilled until crispy. The bread absorbs the meat's juices, resulting in a flavorful and satisfying meal. Hawawshi can be found in street food stalls or restaurants and is perfect for a quick, tasty bite.

Where to try it: Hawawshi El Refaay is known for serving some of the best in Cairo. With generous fillings and perfectly cooked bread, this spot is ideal for those craving a hearty meal.

Egyptian Sweets: A Taste of Tradition

1.Basbousa

A semolina cake soaked in sugar syrup, basbousa is a popular dessert across Egypt. Often topped with almonds or coconut, this sweet treat is dense yet soft, with a texture that melts in your mouth.

Where to try it: El Abd Pastry Shop in downtown Cairo is renowned for its traditional Egyptian sweets, including basbousa. It's a favorite spot for locals picking up treats for special occasions.

2.Kunafa

A Middle Eastern dessert that has made its way into Egyptian hearts, is made from thin, shredded phyllo dough layered with cream or cheese, then soaked in syrup. Crunchy on the outside and soft inside, it's the perfect indulgence.

Where to try it: **Mandarine Koueider** is a well-known patisserie that specializes in , offering both classic and modern versions of this beloved dessert.

3. Om Ali

Considered Egypt's answer to bread pudding, Om Ali is a rich, creamy dessert made from layers of flaky pastry mixed with milk, sugar, and nuts, then baked until golden. It's a decadent dish that's enjoyed warm, often during festive occasions.

Where to try it: Try this delicious dessert at *Cairo Kitchen*, where they serve a modern take on traditional Egyptian cuisine, including Om Ali.

Where to Eat in Cairo: Dining Options for Every Taste

Cairo's food scene is incredibly diverse, catering to both locals and tourists with a range of dining options, from simple street food stalls to high-end restaurants offering contemporary interpretations of Egyptian classics.

1. Street Food

Cairo's street food culture is vibrant, offering a glimpse into everyday Egyptian life. Whether you're grabbing a quick sandwich from a corner vendor or enjoying a bowl of koshari at a bustling stall, street food in Cairo is both affordable and delicious. For an authentic experience, head to **El Sayeda Zainab** OR **El Husseiniya,** where the street food scene is as lively as it gets.

2.Casual Dining

For those looking to sit down and enjoy a traditional meal in a relaxed setting, Cairo offers a range of casual dining options. Restaurants like **Abou El Sid** serve classic Egyptian dishes in an atmosphere that feels like stepping back in time, with vintage decor and an old-world charm.

3.Fine Dining

Cairo also boasts a growing fine dining scene, where chefs are experimenting with contemporary takes on traditional flavors. **Zooba** is a standout example, offering Egyptian street food with a gourmet twist. For those looking to dine with a view, **Sequoia** offers Mediterranean and Egyptian cuisine along the Nile, combining fine dining with beautiful surroundings.

Whether you're exploring Cairo's bustling streets or enjoying a meal overlooking the Nile, Egyptian cuisine offers a delicious and immersive way to experience the country's rich culture and history. The flavors of Egypt, from its hearty street food to its indulgent desserts, reflect the warmth and vibrancy of its people—making every bite a journey in itself.

Street Food in Cairo: Quick Bites and Flavorful Snacks

Cairo's bustling streets offer a sensory feast, with the vibrant aromas of sizzling meat, fresh bread, and spices filling the air. The city's street food scene is an essential part of its cultural identity, providing a taste of authentic Egyptian flavors that are as affordable as they are satisfying. Whether you're wandering through historic alleys, navigating lively markets, or simply taking in the everyday rhythms of the city, these quick bites and snacks are a delicious introduction to Cairo's culinary landscape.

1. *Sambousek*

These golden, fried pastries are the Egyptian version of samosas. **Sambousek** can be stuffed with various fillings, such as spiced meat, cheese, or vegetables, making them a versatile snack that can be found in food stalls across the city. The flaky pastry combined with savory fillings makes sambousek a perfect grab-and-go snack.

Where to try it: You'll find sambousek being sold in busy marketplaces like **Khan El Khalili**, where vendors offer a wide array of flavors to cater to all tastes.

2. *Sweet Potatoes*

If you're walking through Cairo's streets in the cooler months, you're likely to encounter the warm, inviting smell of roasted sweet potatoes. Sold from street carts, these sweet treats are baked over hot coals until tender and caramelized. They're often served split in half, with the soft flesh eaten right from the skin. Simple yet utterly satisfying, roasted sweet potatoes are a comforting snack that warms you from the inside out.

Where to try it: Look for the traditional sweet potato carts in areas like **Zamalek** or along the Nile Corniche.

3. *Fiteer (Egyptian Pie)*

Fiteer, sometimes referred to as Egyptian pizza, is a flaky pastry that can be either savory or sweet. The dough is stretched thin and layered with butter before being baked, resulting in a crispy, buttery pie. Savory versions are filled with cheese, meats, or vegetables, while sweet varieties are topped with honey, nuts, or sugar. Fiteer is a popular street food for those who want a filling and flavorful bite, and it can be shared among friends or family.

Where to try it: For a traditional experience, visit **Fiteer Ghazal**, a renowned bakery in Cairo's **Islamic quarter**, where they serve a variety of both savory and sweet options.

4. Shawarma

Though shawarma is common across the Middle East, Egypt's version has its own unique flair. Layers of marinated meat, often lamb or chicken, are slow-cooked on a vertical spit and shaved off into warm flatbread, then topped with tahini, garlic sauce, pickles, and sometimes fries. The contrast of the juicy meat and the crisp bread makes shawarma a popular option for both lunch and dinner.

Where to try it: For some of the best shawarma in Cairo, check out **Gad**, a local fast-food chain known for serving traditional Egyptian street food at affordable prices.

5. Aish Baladi with Dips

Aish Baladi, the Egyptian flatbread, is a key component of many street food meals. It's made from whole wheat and baked in traditional ovens, often sold warm right off the street. Eaten on its own or with various dips like tahini, baba ganoush, or duqqa (a mix of nuts and spices), is a versatile snack that pairs well with other dishes or serves as a light bite on its own.

Where to try it: Local bakeries throughout Cairo sell freshly baked , but for a real treat, visit **Bakar Bakery** in Giza for some of the freshest bread in the area.

6.*Egyptian Desserts on the Go*

Cairo's streets are also a treasure trove for those with a sweet tooth. **Basbousa**, a semolina cake soaked in syrup, and **Kunafa**, a crispy pastry filled with cream or cheese, are two iconic desserts that you'll find in bakeries and stalls. For a more refreshing option, locals often turn to (sugarcane juice), a sweet and thirst-quenching drink that's sold at carts throughout the city.

Where to try it: **El Abd** Pastry Shop is a great place to sample Egyptian desserts, while street vendors in areas like **Downtown Cairo** sell fresh sugarcane juice to sip as you stroll.

Cairo's street food scene is not just about satisfying hunger; it's an integral part of the city's culture and daily life. Each bite is an opportunity to experience the city's rich culinary history, shaped by centuries of tradition and innovation. From savory to sweet, from light snacks to hearty meals, Cairo's streets are a living menu waiting to be explored. Whether you're on the go or taking your time to enjoy the city's vibrant atmosphere, these flavorful quick bites will leave you with a taste of Egypt that's hard to forget.

Fine Dining and International Restaurants in the City

Cairo's dining scene has evolved into a culinary hub, blending traditional Egyptian flavors with global cuisines. The city boasts a range of upscale, fine-dining establishments and international restaurants, where you can enjoy gourmet dishes crafted by skilled chefs. From elegant, candlelit settings to chic rooftop terraces overlooking the Nile, Cairo's dining options cater to all tastes and preferences..

1.*Sequoia*

Located on the Zamalek island, **Sequoia** is a favorite for those seeking a sophisticated dining experience with stunning views of the Nile. The ambiance is laid-back yet chic, with a diverse menu that features Middle Eastern, Mediterranean, and seafood dishes.

-**Mezze Platter (mixed appetizers)**: 250 EGP($8.10)
-**Grilled Sea Bass**: 450 EGP($14.58)
-**Lamb Chops**: 400 EGP($12.96)
-**Sushi (various rolls)**: 150-400($4.86-$12.96) EGP per roll
-**Signature Cocktail**: 200 EGP($6.48)

The restaurant's location, ambiance, and range of international dishes make it a perfect spot for a leisurely dinner or celebratory meal.

2.*La Bodega*

Nestled in an art-deco building in Zamalek,**La Bodega** offers French and Mediterranean cuisine in an elegant and intimate atmosphere. The restaurant's decor features grand chandeliers, leather armchairs, and antique mirrors, setting the stage for a refined dining experience.

-**Duck Confit**: 350 EGP($11.34)

-**Grilled Salmon with Lemon Butter Sauce**: 450 EGP($14.58)
-**Filet Mignon with Red Wine Sauce**: 550 EGP($17.82)
-**French Onion Soup**: 180 EGP($5.83)
-**Crème Brûlée**: 150 EGP($4.86)

La Bodega is a great choice for those seeking French-inspired cuisine paired with expertly curated wines.

3.*The Grill at the Four Seasons*
Located within the luxurious **Four Seasons Hotel Cairo** at Nile Plaza, **The Grill** is a sophisticated French restaurant offering elegant dishes and impeccable service. Diners can enjoy beautiful Nile views while sampling gourmet cuisine made with the freshest ingredients.

-**Foie Gras with Brioche:** 480 EGP($15.55)
-**Beef Tenderloin:** 800 EGP($25.92)
-**Lobster Thermidor**: 1,200 EGP($38.88)
-**Truffle Risotto:** 500 EGP($16.20)
-**French Pastries (assortment):** 300 EGP($9.72)

Known for its chic atmosphere and exquisite dishes, The Grill provides a premier fine dining experience in Cairo.

4. *Sachi*

Sachi is a contemporary fine dining spot located in Heliopolis, offering a blend of Mediterranean, Japanese, and international cuisines. The restaurant is well-known for its stylish, modern design and diverse menu, making it popular among Cairo's elite.

-**Tuna Tartar**: 350 EGP($11.34)
-**Black Cod Miso**: 800 EGP($25.92)
-**Wagyu Beef Steak**: 1,100 EGP($35.64)
-**Signature Sushi Rolls**: 250-600 EGP per roll($8.10)
-**Chocolate Fondant**: 180 EGP($5.83)

Sachi's sophisticated atmosphere and artistic presentations make it a top choice for special occasions or intimate dinners.

5.Pier 88

Floating atop the Nile, **Pier 88** in Zamalek offers upscale Mediterranean cuisine in a trendy, minimalist setting. With a sleek design and a menu focused on fresh ingredients, Pier 88 has become a popular spot for both locals and visitors looking for a vibrant yet refined dining experience.

- **Seafood Linguine:** 550 EGP($17.82)
- **Grilled Octopus:** 400 EGP($12.96)
- **Prime Ribeye Steak:** 850 EGP($27.54)
- **Burrata Salad:** 300 EGP($9.72)
- **Mojito:** 200 EGP($6.48)

With its stylish ambiance and creative Mediterranean dishes, Pier 88 provides an exclusive dining experience with panoramic views of the Nile.

6. *Zitouni*

Also located within the **Four Seasons Nile Plaza**, **Zitouni** is a modern Egyptian restaurant serving authentic local dishes with a contemporary twist. Diners can enjoy the finest traditional Egyptian flavors, prepared with premium ingredients and presented in an upscale setting.

- **Molokhia with Chicken:** 350 EGP($11.34)
- **Koshari (signature twist:** 250 EGP($8.10)
- **Roast Pigeon with Freekeh:** 400 EGP($12.96)
- **Grilled Kofta:** 300 EGP($9.72)
- **Baklava with Honey:** 150 EGP($4.86)

For those looking to experience Egyptian cuisine in a luxurious setting, Zitouni offers a modern take on traditional dishes.

7. *Kazoku*

Located in **New Cairo**, **Kazoku** is a sophisticated Japanese restaurant offering a high-end sushi and robata grill experience. The chic design, combined with meticulously crafted dishes, makes Kazoku a standout in Cairo's dining scene.

- **Sashimi Platter:** 750 EGP($24.30)
- **Grilled Wagyu Short Rib:** 1,200 EGP($38.88)
- **Miso Black Cod:** 850 EGP($27.54)
- **Ebi Tempura Roll:** 300 EGP($9.72)
- **Matcha Ice Cream:** 180 EGP($5.83)

Kazoku's sleek, modern design and premium Japanese offerings make it an essential stop for sushi lovers and fine-dining enthusiasts.

8. *JW's Steakhouse*

Housed in the **Cairo Marriott Hotel**, **JW's Steakhouse** is a luxurious choice for those seeking expertly cooked steaks and a sophisticated dining atmosphere. The restaurant prides itself on serving prime cuts of meat with a variety of classic accompaniments.

- **Australian Wagyu Ribeye:** 1,200 EGP($38.88)
- **Grilled Lamb Chops:** 650 EGP($21.06)

-**Surf & Turf:** 950 EGP($30.78)
-**Baked Potato with Sour Cream:** 100 EGP($3.24)
-**New York Cheesecake:** 200 EGP($6.48)

JW's Steakhouse delivers a classic steakhouse experience with an elegant Egyptian twist, perfect for a night of indulgence.

Cairo's fine dining and international restaurant scene reflect its growing status as a global metropolis. With a mixture of elegant settings, creative dishes, and international flavors, the city's culinary landscape is sure to cater to diverse tastes and offer unforgettable dining experiences. Whether you're in the mood for Japanese delicacies, Mediterranean freshness, or traditional Egyptian feasts, Cairo's restaurants have something to offer for every occasion and palate.

Chapter Six

Cairo by Night: Entertainment and Nightlife

Rooftop Bars and Lounges with Nile Views

Cairo's nightlife offers a vibrant mix of experiences, and one of the most enjoyable ways to unwind after a day of exploring is by visiting one of the city's rooftop bars or lounges. These elevated spots, perched high above the bustling streets, offer stunning views of the Nile River, merging the energy of modern Cairo with the calm of its legendary waterway. Whether you're looking for a quiet drink at sunset or a lively evening with friends, these venues showcase a blend of Egyptian hospitality, contemporary flair, and incredible vistas.

The Terrace Experience

Rooftop terraces in Cairo offer a unique vantage point to witness the city come to life. As the sun dips below the horizon, the Nile shimmers, reflecting the fading light while the skyline glows with energy. Many of these lounges are located on top of high-end hotels, providing a sophisticated atmosphere where you can enjoy cocktails, local dishes, and international cuisine. The terraces often combine sleek, modern décor with touches of traditional Egyptian design, creating a setting that feels both exclusive and relaxed. These rooftop spaces are popular among locals and travelers alike, offering a refuge from the city's fast-paced rhythm while embracing its unique character.

The Revolving Nile Ritz-Carlton Lounge

Perhaps one of the most luxurious rooftop spots in the city, the Nile Ritz-Carlton's rooftop lounge combines modern elegance with unparalleled views of the river. The bar's revolving aspect ensures you're treated to a 360-degree view of Cairo, from the sweeping Nile to the illuminated cityscape. Whether enjoying a signature cocktail or a fine glass of wine, this venue caters to those seeking an upscale experience. The setting is intimate, making it ideal for both romantic evenings and small gatherings. Prices here reflect the high-end experience, with drinks starting around 150 EGP ($5) and rising depending on your selection.

The Rooftop at Kempinski Nile Hotel

The Kempinski Nile Hotel offers a stylish and contemporary rooftop bar with a breathtaking panorama of the Nile. Known for its expertly crafted cocktails and gourmet bites, this venue attracts a fashionable crowd. The combination of soft lighting, plush seating, and views that stretch for miles creates an ambiance that invites relaxation. For those looking to dine, the rooftop also serves a selection of Mediterranean-inspired dishes, blending flavors with the fresh breeze from the Nile. Expect to pay around 200 to 250 EGP ($6.50 to $8) for a cocktail, with meals ranging from 300 EGP ($9.75) for lighter options to 600 EGP ($19.50) for full-course meals.

Crimson Bar & Grill

Located in the affluent district of Zamalek, Crimson Bar & Grill offers a more laid-back yet stylish experience. The atmosphere is both modern and comfortable, with wooden decking and casual seating that overlooks the shimmering Nile. Known for its extensive wine list and craft cocktails, this rooftop bar strikes a perfect balance between casual dining and nightlife. Visitors can enjoy signature Egyptian mezze, alongside contemporary international dishes. Prices are moderate, with cocktails averaging 180 to 250 EGP

($5.85 to $8.10), while dinner for two can range from 600 to 900 EGP ($19.50 to $29.25).

RoofTop Zamalek

Zamalek, an island district known for its cultural and artistic appeal, is home to another gem—RoofTop Zamalek. This venue provides panoramic views of the Nile and the cityscape. It's chic, minimalist design emphasizes comfort and open spaces, offering a relaxed setting where you can enjoy a refreshing drink or an evening meal. The menu offers a wide variety of both local and international dishes, while the drink selection features signature cocktails crafted with local ingredients. Visitors praise the reasonable prices, with drinks starting at around 120 EGP ($3.90) and meals from 250 EGP ($8.10).

Le Deck by Laurent Peugeot

For those seeking a blend of fine dining and stunning views, Le Deck, located on a floating platform along the Nile, is a standout option. Though not a rooftop, its open-air setting offers a similarly striking perspective of the river and Cairo's skyline. Led by Michelin-starred chef Laurent Peugeot, the restaurant's cuisine fuses French techniques with Asian flavors, offering a distinctive culinary experience. Prices reflect the upscale nature, with dishes starting at 500 EGP ($16.20), while a cocktail can cost around 250 EGP ($8.10). Le Deck is perfect for a sophisticated evening out, combining gourmet dining with the tranquility of Nile views.

Sky Executive Lounge at Conrad Cairo
Set within the Conrad Cairo Hotel, the Sky Executive Lounge provides an atmosphere of elegance and exclusivity. Offering stunning views of the river and downtown Cairo, this rooftop venue caters to those who prefer a quieter, more refined environment. With an extensive menu of premium cocktails, international wines, and gourmet snacks, this is a go-to for those seeking a more intimate experience. Prices are on the higher side, with cocktails averaging around 200 EGP ($6.48) and tapas-style plates starting at 250 EGP ($8.10).

Evening Vibes: Music and Atmosphere
Many of Cairo's rooftop bars and lounges also serve as hubs for live entertainment. From smooth jazz to modern electronic music, these venues feature a range of musical styles that enhance the atmosphere without overwhelming the experience. The combination of music, stunning views, and expertly crafted drinks creates an

inviting space for a memorable night out in Cairo. For example, Crimson Bar & Grill often hosts live DJs, adding a vibrant energy as the evening progresses.

Whether you're sipping on a cocktail while watching the sunset or enjoying a gourmet meal under the stars, Cairo's rooftop bars and lounges offer unforgettable experiences. The stunning views of the Nile and the city's skyline, combined with a diverse range of dining and drink options, make these spots a must for anyone visiting the city. Each venue brings its own flair, whether through luxurious settings, casual vibes, or intimate atmospheres, ensuring that there's a rooftop experience for every kind of traveler.

Traditional Music and Dance: Experience Egyptian Folklore

Egyptian folklore is a deep well of cultural expression, passed down through generations, reflecting the country's rich history, diverse regions, and the blending of ancient and modern influences. Traditional music and dance have always been central to Egyptian life, offering a glimpse into the soul of the nation. Whether through the haunting melodies of ancient instruments, the rhythmic movements of folkloric dance, or the lively celebrations at cultural festivals, Egypt's folklore is an experience not to be missed.

The Heartbeat of Egypt: Traditional Music

Egyptian traditional music is as diverse as its landscape. Over centuries, it has been influenced by ancient Pharaonic traditions, Islamic culture, and even interactions with Mediterranean, African, and Middle Eastern societies. At its core are instruments that have remained largely unchanged through time, creating sounds that feel both ancient and alive.

-*The Oud:* This pear-shaped, stringed instrument is a cornerstone of Egyptian music. Often described as the ancestor of the modern guitar, the oud produces rich, melodious tones that evoke a sense of timelessness. Its sound is most commonly heard in classical Egyptian music, but also in contemporary compositions, blending old and new worlds.

-*The Ney:* The ney, a long, reed flute, has been used in Egyptian music for over 5,000 years, with depictions found in tomb paintings and ancient carvings. Its breathy, ethereal sound creates a haunting, melancholic mood that is often used to accompany poetry, spiritual music, and storytelling performances.

-**The Tabla and Dof**: The tabla (a goblet-shaped drum) and dof (a larger frame drum) provide the rhythmic backbone of Egyptian music. They are essential to Egyptian folk music, with lively, complex rhythms that reflect the heartbeat of village life, celebrations, and traditional dances.

-**The Rababa:** The , a simple stringed instrument made from wood, metal, and animal skin, is central to rural Egyptian music. It is commonly used in storytelling, particularly in Upper Egypt, where musicians (known as **Al-Shu'ara**) play it to accompany ancient epics and tales of heroes.

Folkloric Dance: Movement That Tells a Story

Egyptian dance traditions are vast, reflecting the country's regional diversity and historical richness. While most people associate Egypt with the visually stunning movements of belly dance (sharqi), there are a variety of other folkloric dances deeply rooted in specific areas and customs of the country.

-**Raqs Baladi**: Literally meaning "dance of the people," is a form of Egyptian folk dance that originates from rural villages. This style of dance is often performed by women during community celebrations and family gatherings, featuring grounded, rhythmic movements that celebrate life, fertility, and feminine strength.

-*Tanoura*: One of Egypt's most mesmerizing dance forms, the **tanoura** dance comes from Sufi traditions and is performed by dervishes as a spiritual practice. Dressed in brightly colored skirts, the dancers spin continuously in circles to the beat of live music, symbolizing the eternal cycle of life and the soul's journey toward unity with the divine. The hypnotic twirl of the dancers, paired with the melodic hum of traditional instruments, makes for an unforgettable spectacle.

-*Saidi Dance*: Originating from Upper Egypt, the **Saidi** dance is one of the most well-known folkloric dance forms in Egypt. Typically performed by men, this dance involves vigorous, energetic movements, often featuring a wooden cane (known as **Assaya**), which the dancers twirl and spin to demonstrate strength and agility. It is accompanied by lively traditional music and can also be adapted into female performances with more delicate, playful interpretations.

-**Nubian Dance:** In Egypt's southern regions, Nubian dance plays an important role in maintaining cultural identity. Performed during weddings and festivals, Nubian dance involves joyous group performances where men and women participate in vibrant, synchronized movements, accompanied by traditional songs that reflect their unique heritage. The bright, colorful costumes and rhythmic steps of this dance offer an entirely different flavor of Egyptian folklore.

Festivals and Cultural Events: Folklore Comes to Life

Experiencing Egyptian traditional music and dance at one of the many cultural festivals across the country is a true immersion into its vibrant heritage. These festivals bring communities together and showcase Egypt's folklore on a grand stage, making it accessible to both locals and visitors.

-**Moulid Festivals**: One of the best opportunities to experience Egyptian folklore is during **moulids**, or religious festivals, held in honor of saints and holy figures. These celebrations, which take place in cities and villages across the country, are vibrant, joyous occasions filled with music, dance, and communal activities. Traditional music, especially that played on the rabab and tabla, is integral to these events, while dances like the **tanoura** often take center stage.

-*The International Festival for Drums and Traditional Arts*: Held annually in Cairo, this festival draws performers from across Egypt and beyond, bringing together the rhythmic sounds of the tabla and dof with the diverse drumming traditions of other cultures. It is a wonderful opportunity to see traditional Egyptian dance forms alongside international acts, making it a cultural melting pot of folklore and heritage.

-*The El Gouna Film and Music Festival*: Though a more modern cultural event, this festival, held along the Red Sea, often includes performances that highlight Egyptian folklore, particularly in its opening and closing ceremonies. With music, dance, and celebrations of Egypt's artistic heritage, it's a showcase of how folklore continues to influence contemporary culture.

Where to Experience Folklore in Cairo

For those staying in Cairo and eager to experience traditional Egyptian music and dance, there are several venues where folklore performances are regularly held.

-**Wekalet El Ghouri Arts Center**: Located in the heart of Islamic Cairo, this center is one of the most famous places to experience traditional Sufi music and **tanoura** performances. The energy of the spinning dervishes, accompanied by live music, is unforgettable. The weekly performances are popular with both locals and tourists, offering an authentic glimpse into Egypt's mystical traditions.

-**El Sawy Culture Wheel**: A hub for both contemporary and traditional arts, this venue often hosts performances of Egyptian folkloric music and dance. Located on Zamalek island, it provides a perfect setting to experience everything from Nubian dance to **Saidi** music, making it a great spot for those looking to dive into Egypt's folk heritage.

Traditional music and dance are more than just entertainment in Egypt; they are an expression of its soul. Whether you're witnessing a spirited **Saidi** dance, losing yourself in the rhythm of a **tanoura** performance, or hearing the ancient tones of the oud and ney, Egyptian folklore connects the past with the present in a way that few other cultural expressions can. Experiencing it firsthand is a powerful reminder of the enduring power of art, music, and tradition in shaping a nation's identity.

Cafés and Hookah Spots: Relax in Cairo's Evening Breeze

Cairo's vibrant café culture and traditional hookah spots offer a unique glimpse into the social heart of the city. Whether you're looking for a laid-back spot to sip tea or coffee while people-watching, or a cozy nook to enjoy the timeless tradition of smoking a **shisha** (hookah), Cairo's streets come alive in the evening as locals and visitors alike gather to unwind. The warmth of Cairo's evening breeze, paired with the rich aromas of brewing coffee and sweet shisha smoke, creates an atmosphere that is both relaxed and lively.

The Quintessential Cairo Café Experience

Cairo's cafés are an integral part of the city's social fabric, offering more than just food and drink. These spaces serve as gathering spots for friends, intellectuals, and travelers, making them places of conversation, contemplation, and community.

Whether you're strolling through the bustling downtown streets or exploring the quieter alleys of Old Cairo, you'll find a diverse selection of cafés, each with its own character and charm.

-**Café Riche**: One of the oldest and most famous cafés in Cairo, Café Riche has been a meeting place for intellectuals, artists, and revolutionaries for over a century. Located in Downtown Cairo, its old-world charm, complete with wooden furnishings and vintage décor, makes it a cozy escape from the busy streets outside. Whether you're in for a cup of Turkish coffee or a light meal, Café Riche offers an authentic taste of Cairo's café culture.

-**El Fishawy Café**: Nestled in the heart of Khan El Khalili Bazaar, El Fishawy is one of Cairo's most iconic cafés. Established over 200 years ago, this café is a bustling spot frequented by locals and tourists alike. It's an ideal place to enjoy a cup of mint tea or (Arabic coffee) while absorbing the vibrant surroundings of the bazaar. The café's narrow alley setting, adorned with mirrors and vintage furniture, adds to the experience, and its reputation as a favorite haunt of famous Egyptian writers only enhances its allure.

-**Qahwa**: For a more modern twist on Cairo's café scene, Qahwa, located in the upscale Zamalek district, offers a chic setting with a blend of traditional and contemporary influences. This café specializes in gourmet coffee blends and offers an extensive menu of snacks and desserts. Its relaxed ambiance makes it a perfect spot for those seeking a quieter evening in the city.

Hookah Spots: The Art of Relaxation

The tradition of smoking **shisha** is deeply rooted in Egyptian culture, with hookah cafés scattered throughout Cairo's neighborhoods. These establishments range from traditional venues steeped in history to more modern, trendy spots that cater to younger crowds. No matter where you go, the experience of smoking **shisha** while engaging in lively conversation is a quintessential part of Cairo's evening life.

-**Naguib Mahfouz Café**: Another Khan El Khalili gem, this café offers both delicious food and a traditional hookah experience. Named after Egypt's Nobel Prize-winning novelist, Naguib Mahfouz Café provides an atmospheric blend of history, literature, and tradition. With its dimly lit, intricately designed interior, it's an excellent spot to relax with a **shisha** while reflecting on the works of Mahfouz or simply enjoying the hum of the bazaar outside.

-**Al-Horreya Café**: Located in Downtown Cairo, Al-Horreya has long been a favorite spot for artists, intellectuals, and students. Known for its no-frills approach, this café is a relic of Cairo's past, where the emphasis is on socializing rather than luxury. Here, patrons gather around large wooden tables, order simple drinks, and share **shisha** as they debate everything from politics to poetry. The open windows let in the cool evening breeze, adding to the relaxed, almost timeless atmosphere.

-**Zizo Café:** Situated in the neighborhood of Mohandessin, Zizo Café is a more contemporary take on the traditional hookah spot. With its vibrant atmosphere, modern décor, and a varied menu of **shisha** flavors, this café attracts a younger, trendier crowd. It's a perfect place for groups to gather in the evening, enjoying a mix of traditional and modern Cairo life while smoking **shisha** in style.

<u>Relaxing in the Evening Breeze: A Cairo Tradition</u>
Cairo's evenings are defined by a slower, more relaxed pace, where the warm breeze carries the

scent of street food and **shisha** smoke. As the sun sets over the Nile and the day's hustle quiets down, these cafés and hookah spots become the focal points of social life. It's here that conversations flow, friendships are nurtured, and the city's rich cultural history continues to evolve.

In many ways, the experience of sitting in a Cairo café or hookah spot is about more than just the coffee or the **shisha**. It's about being part of the city's rhythm, immersing yourself in its stories, and connecting with its people. Whether you're tucked away in a quiet corner of a historic café or enjoying the vibrant energy of a modern hookah lounge, these spaces offer a true taste of Cairo's timeless charm.

Chapter Seven

Beyond the City: Day Trips and Excursions

Alexandria: A Coastal Escape from Cairo

As you step out of Cairo's bustling streets, Alexandria offers a refreshing change of pace with its Mediterranean charm and coastal beauty. Egypt's second-largest city, Alexandria has a distinctly different atmosphere, blending a rich historical legacy with a more relaxed, seaside vibe. Situated just over two hours from Cairo by car or train, Alexandria is an ideal escape for those seeking to experience the best of Egypt's coastal treasures while still immersed in the country's profound history and culture.

A Historical Port City with a Mediterranean Soul

Founded by Alexander the Great in 331 BC, Alexandria was once the capital of Egypt and a renowned center of learning and culture. The city's historical significance is intertwined with its famous library, the Great Lighthouse of Pharos (one of the Seven Wonders of the Ancient World), and its legacy as a hub of intellectualism and commerce in the ancient world. Today, while much of its ancient grandeur has faded,

Alexandria still retains an undeniable air of elegance, with its blend of old-world architecture, picturesque harbors, and vibrant cultural life.

Strolling through Alexandria, you'll encounter a mix of Greco-Roman ruins, grand 19th-century buildings, and modern developments, all framed by the tranquil blue waters of the Mediterranean Sea. The city's history isn't just confined to the past; it weaves seamlessly into the modern fabric of Alexandria, making it a living museum where the ancient and the contemporary sit side by side.

The Corniche: A Seafront Promenade
No visit to Alexandria is complete without a leisurely walk along the Corniche, the city's famous waterfront promenade. Stretching for miles along the coastline, the Corniche offers stunning views of the Mediterranean, with the sea breeze providing a welcome respite from the heat. As you stroll, you'll pass by historical landmarks, traditional cafés, and elegant hotels, all set against the backdrop of the shimmering sea.

The Corniche is the perfect place to experience Alexandria's relaxed coastal lifestyle. Whether you're stopping for a cup of coffee at a seaside café, watching local fishermen cast their nets, or simply taking in the views, this promenade captures the essence of Alexandria as a city that thrives on its connection to the sea.

Montazah Palace Gardens: A Royal Retreat

Nestled along the eastern edge of the city, the Montazah Palace Gardens provide a peaceful escape from the urban bustle. Originally built as a royal retreat, the palace grounds are now open to the public, offering expansive gardens filled with palm trees, flowers, and walking paths. The Montaza Palace itself, with its blend of Ottoman and Florentine architecture, stands as a reminder of Alexandria's regal past.

The gardens offer a serene setting to relax, take a picnic, or simply enjoy the lush greenery that contrasts with the arid desert landscapes of much of Egypt. The nearby Montazah Beach, with its golden sands and gentle waves, is a favorite spot for swimming and sunbathing, adding to the area's appeal as a peaceful coastal getaway.

Ancient Wonders: From the Bibliotheca Alexandrina to Catacombs

Though much of ancient Alexandria has been lost to time, the city's historical sites remain among its biggest draws. The **Bibliotheca Alexandrina**, a modern-day tribute to the ancient Library of Alexandria, is a state-of-the-art cultural and research center. Its striking architecture, featuring a giant tilted disc representing the sun, houses millions of books, art galleries, museums, and exhibition spaces. Visiting the Bibliotheca not only offers a chance to explore Alexandria's rich intellectual heritage but also provides insight into its modern cultural revival.

Another must-see is the **Catacombs of Kom El Shoqafa**, an impressive ancient burial site that dates back to the 2nd century AD. The catacombs are a labyrinth of tunnels and chambers, with unique decorations that blend Egyptian, Greek, and Roman influences. As you descend into the depths of these underground tombs, you'll feel transported back to an era when Alexandria was a cultural melting pot of civilizations.

Fort Qaitbay: Guardian of the Mediterranean
Located at the tip of the Eastern Harbor, **Fort Qaitbay** stands as a sentinel overlooking the sea. Built in the 15th century by Sultan Al-Ashraf Sayf al-Din Qa'it Bay, the fort was constructed on the site of the ancient Pharos Lighthouse. While the original wonder of the world was destroyed by earthquakes centuries ago, Fort Qaitbay's sturdy

stone walls have weathered time and offer stunning views of the Mediterranean coastline.

Inside the fort, visitors can explore its towers and chambers, imagining life as a soldier defending the city from invaders. The fort's strategic position, surrounded by the sea on three sides, provides panoramic vistas that capture the beauty and power of the Mediterranean.

<u>Alexandria's Food Scene: Fresh Seafood and Local Flavors</u>
Alexandria's coastal location means that seafood is at the heart of its culinary scene. The city's fish markets, such as the bustling **Anfushi Market**, offer fresh catches straight from the Mediterranean, and many of Alexandria's restaurants specialize in serving up these delights.

-**Fish Market Restaurant:** This popular waterfront restaurant offers stunning views of the harbor along with a menu filled with fresh fish, calamari, shrimp, and lobster. Prices vary depending on the day's catch, but the quality and flavor are unmatched.

-**Taverna**: For a mix of Mediterranean and Egyptian cuisine, Taverna in the city center serves up a variety of seafood dishes as well as traditional mezze and grilled meats. It's a favorite for both locals and visitors alike.

-**Abou Ashraf:** Located near the Corniche, Abou Ashraf is known for its no-frills atmosphere and incredible seafood platters. Here, you'll find grilled fish, shrimp, and calamari served with local bread and rice for a truly authentic Alexandrian meal.

A Coastal Escape with Rich Heritage
Alexandria is more than just a seaside escape; it's a city that pulses with history, culture, and the salty air of the Mediterranean. From its ancient ruins and royal gardens to its vibrant Corniche and bustling markets, Alexandria offers travelers a rich blend of experiences just a short journey from Cairo. Whether you're exploring the remnants of its storied past or simply enjoying a sunset over the Mediterranean, Alexandria provides a coastal getaway that's steeped in both relaxation and discovery.

The Fayoum Oasis: Nature and History Combined
Nestled just a couple of hours southwest of Cairo, the **Fayoum Oasis** offers a perfect escape from the

hustle and bustle of the capital, blending Egypt's stunning natural beauty with its deep historical roots. Known for its rich landscapes, ancient ruins, and serene lakes, Fayoum provides a more laid-back, yet deeply enriching experience for travelers seeking to explore Egypt's rural heartland. It's a place where nature and history are inseparable, creating a destination that's ideal for adventure, relaxation, and exploration.

A Natural Haven: Lakes, Waterfalls, and Desert Dunes

Fayoum is most famous for **Lake Qarun**, Egypt's largest saltwater lake, which sits at the heart of the oasis. This ancient lake, known as the "Lake of Moeris" in antiquity, has been a lifeline for the region for thousands of years. Today, it remains a tranquil spot for picnics, bird-watching, and fishing. Flamingos, pelicans, and other migratory birds can often be spotted wading in the shallow waters, particularly during the winter months, making it a paradise for nature lovers and ornithologists.

Beyond the lake lies **Wadi El-Rayan,** a protected nature reserve known for its spectacular waterfalls—the only waterfalls in Egypt. Here, the waters cascade from one lake to another, surrounded by desert dunes and rocky cliffs. The reserve is a stunning example of the contrast between Egypt's arid desert and its lush oases. Visitors can swim in the cool waters of the lakes, hike the surrounding terrain, or even embark on a thrilling sandboarding adventure down the nearby dunes.

For those seeking more solitude, **Wadi El-Hitan**, or the "Valley of the Whales," offers a surreal experience. This UNESCO World Heritage Site is home to an extraordinary collection of fossilized whale skeletons, remnants of a time when this desert was submerged under a prehistoric sea. The fossils, some over 40 million years old, are displayed amidst the rugged desert, a testament to the ancient forces that shaped the land.

Ancient History and Archaeological Wonders
Fayoum's natural beauty is matched by its historical significance, with a legacy that stretches back to the earliest days of Egyptian civilization. The region has been inhabited for millennia, and its archaeological treasures are a testament to its long-standing role as a cultural and agricultural hub.

One of the most important historical sites in the area is **Karanis**, an ancient Greco-Roman town located near Lake Qarun. Once a bustling city, Karanis now lies in ruins, with crumbling temples, homes, and public buildings providing a glimpse into life during the Ptolemaic and Roman periods. The ruins are scattered across the desert, offering a hauntingly beautiful landscape for exploration.

Hawara Pyramid, built by Pharaoh Amenemhat III during the Middle Kingdom, is another must-see for history enthusiasts. Although not as well-known as the Pyramids of Giza, the Hawara Pyramid is an important part of Egypt's architectural legacy. Nearby, the **Labyrinth**, which was once described by the ancient Greek historian Herodotus as a monumental structure of countless chambers and corridors, remains shrouded in mystery. Though little of the labyrinth survives today, the site continues to intrigue archaeologists and visitors alike.

Qasr Qarun, located near the western edge of Lake Qarun, is a well-preserved temple from the Ptolemaic period, dedicated to the crocodile god Sobek. This sandstone temple, standing in stark contrast to the surrounding desert, provides panoramic views of the oasis and the lake, making it an ideal stop for history buffs and photographers alike.

Fayoum's Traditional Villages and Local Life

In addition to its natural and historical sites, Fayoum is home to a number of traditional villages where life moves at a slower, more peaceful pace. Visiting these villages offers travelers an opportunity to experience Egypt's rural culture and warm hospitality firsthand.

The village of **Tunis**, perched on a hill overlooking Lake Qarun, has become famous for its pottery. Local artisans produce beautifully crafted ceramics using traditional methods, and the village is dotted with pottery workshops where visitors can watch the craftsmen at work or even try their hand at shaping clay. Tunis is also home to a number of charming guesthouses, making it a popular spot for those wishing to stay overnight and enjoy the oasis at a more leisurely pace.

Wandering through the streets of Fayoum's villages, you'll encounter farmers working in the fields, families tending to their homes, and children playing in the streets, all set against a backdrop of palm trees and water channels that crisscross the fertile landscape. The region's agriculture thrives thanks to the ancient system of irrigation, known as **Bahr Yussef**, which has nourished Fayoum's farmlands for centuries.

Adventure and Outdoor Activities

For the adventurous traveler, Fayoum offers a wide range of outdoor activities. In addition to sandboarding at Wadi El-Rayan, the surrounding desert is ideal for 4x4 safaris, camel trekking, and horseback riding. Whether you're racing across the sand dunes or taking a slow ride through the countryside, the wide-open landscapes provide a sense of freedom and adventure.

Birdwatching is another popular activity, especially around Lake Qarun and Wadi El-Rayan. The region attracts a wide variety of bird species, particularly in the cooler months, making it a prime destination for nature enthusiasts.

For those seeking a more relaxed experience, Fayoum's natural beauty can be enjoyed at a slower pace. Sunset boat rides on Lake Qarun, quiet walks along the shores, and stargazing in the desert are just a few of the peaceful activities that make the oasis an ideal retreat from the noise and heat of the city.

A Timeless Oasis of Nature and Culture

Fayoum offers travelers a unique opportunity to experience Egypt's natural and historical riches in one place. Whether you're exploring ancient ruins, relaxing by a lake, or venturing into the desert, the oasis provides a diverse range of experiences that cater to every type of traveler. With its blend of archaeological wonders, stunning landscapes, and traditional villages, Fayoum is a destination that feels both timeless and distinctly Egyptian.

For those visiting Cairo, Fayoum is more than just a day trip—it's a journey into Egypt's natural beauty and cultural heritage, offering a rare combination of history, adventure, and serenity.

The Temples of Luxor: A Journey Through Time

Luxor, often referred to as the world's greatest open-air museum, is a city where the past seems to intertwine with the present. Nestled along the eastern banks of the Nile River, Luxor is home to some of Egypt's most iconic and historically significant temples, offering visitors an unparalleled journey through the country's ancient legacy. These grand structures have withstood the test of time, standing as a testament to the architectural prowess, spiritual devotion, and artistic mastery of the ancient Egyptians. A visit to the temples of Luxor is not merely a step into history, but a walk among the gods, pharaohs, and civilizations that shaped one of the greatest empires in human history.

Luxor Temple: A Testament to Kings and Gods

Situated in the heart of Luxor, the **Luxor Temple** is a striking symbol of the grandeur and spiritual importance that ancient Thebes (modern-day Luxor) held. Unlike many temples dedicated to a single deity, Luxor Temple is unique in its dedication to the rejuvenation of kingship. Built largely by Amenhotep III and later expanded by Ramses II, the temple was a focal point for the annual Opet Festival, a celebration where the statues of Amun, Mut, and Khonsu were paraded down the Nile from nearby Karnak Temple to Luxor.

The **entrance to the temple,** marked by a towering pylon built by Ramses II, is flanked by colossal statues of the king and a lone obelisk. Originally, two obelisks stood at the entrance, but one was given to France in the 19th century and now resides in the Place de la Concorde in Paris. Walking through the grand entrance, visitors are immediately struck by the vast open courtyards and towering columns that lead deeper into the temple, each intricately carved with scenes of gods, kings, and religious rituals.

At night, Luxor Temple takes on a mystical atmosphere as it is beautifully illuminated, allowing visitors to experience the temple in the cool evening air and imagine the splendor of ancient festivals that once filled its walls.

Karnak Temple: A City of Temples

Just a short distance north of Luxor Temple lies the vast **Karnak Temple Complex**, one of the most awe-inspiring religious sites in the world. Spanning over 200 acres, Karnak was the principal religious center of the god Amun-Ra, and it grew over 2,000 years as successive pharaohs added to its grandeur. What makes Karnak so special is its scale and the diversity of its structures, ranging from massive temples to small chapels and sacred lakes, all dedicated to various gods and aspects of Egyptian spirituality.

The centerpiece of Karnak is the **Great Hypostyle Hall**, an architectural marvel consisting of 134 colossal columns that once supported a stone roof. The hall's sheer size and the intricate carvings that adorn the columns leave visitors in awe, as they walk beneath the towering structures that seem to touch the sky. Each pharaoh left their mark here, inscribing their achievements and devotion to Amun on the walls and columns, creating a tapestry of history that spans generations.

A highlight of any visit to Karnak is the **Sacred Lake**, a large rectangular body of water that was used for religious purification rituals. The lake, surrounded by remnants of ancient buildings, provides a peaceful contrast to the grandeur of the temple structures, offering a serene spot to reflect on the immense history of the site.

Karnak is not just a temple; it's an entire city of temples, and exploring its vast expanse can easily take a full day. As you walk among the ruins, it's easy to imagine the thousands of priests, workers, and worshippers who once filled these sacred grounds.

The Avenue of Sphinxes: A Sacred Pathway
Connecting **Luxor Temple** and **Karnak Temple** is the recently restored **Avenue of Sphinxes**, a 2.7-kilometer road flanked by hundreds of stone sphinxes that once led pilgrims from one temple to another. This grand avenue was rediscovered and excavated after being buried for centuries under modern buildings. Walking along the avenue today is like retracing the steps of the

ancient Egyptians who traveled this route during religious festivals. It is a remarkable symbol of the grandeur and unity between Luxor and Karnak, reflecting the religious significance of the entire region.

Medinet Habu: The Mortuary Temple of Ramses III

On the west bank of the Nile, opposite Luxor, lies **Medinet Habu,** the **Mortuary Temple of Ramses III,** Although less famous than Luxor and Karnak, Medinet Habu is one of the most beautifully preserved temples in Egypt, with vivid reliefs and inscriptions that recount the victories of Ramses III, particularly his battles against the Sea Peoples. The temple's towering walls and impressive pylon depict scenes of warfare and triumph, illustrating the might and authority of the king.

Medinet Habu also served as a major administrative center during Ramses III's reign, and its surrounding buildings once housed offices, storehouses, and living quarters. The temple is a fascinating blend of religious and political power, showcasing both the divine connection of the pharaoh and his role as the protector of Egypt.

The Temples of the West Bank: Valley of the Kings and Mortuary Temples

Luxor's west bank is home to some of Egypt's most famous sites, including the **Valley of the Kings**, where pharaohs were buried in tombs filled with treasures for the afterlife, and the **Mortuary Temple of Hatshepsut**, a stunning terraced temple built into the cliffs at Deir el-Bahari.

The **Valley of the Kings** is where you'll find the tomb of **Tutankhamun**, among others, while the **Temple of Hatshepsut** is a testament to the architectural innovation of the New Kingdom. Both sites are must-visit locations for anyone interested in the funerary practices of ancient Egypt and the powerful connection between the pharaohs and the gods.

The temples of Luxor are not just architectural marvels; they are a living history of Egypt's ancient civilization. Each temple tells its own story—of gods worshiped, kings celebrated, and battles fought. Together, they form an extraordinary journey through time, offering modern visitors a chance to walk in the footsteps of pharaohs, priests, and ordinary citizens who once filled these sacred spaces.

Visiting the temples of Luxor is an experience like no other, one that captures the imagination and transports you to a world where the divine and the earthly were intertwined. Whether you are drawn by the spiritual significance, the historical importance, or the sheer beauty of the temples, Luxor promises an unforgettable encounter with Egypt's rich heritage.

Chapter Eight

Staying in Cairo: Accommodation Options
Luxury Hotels: Where History Meets Comfort

Cairo offers an unparalleled blend of ancient heritage and modern elegance, with its luxury hotels reflecting the rich cultural history while providing all the comforts of modern hospitality. Staying in one of Cairo's top-tier hotels means not only enjoying world-class amenities but also immersing yourself in the historical ambiance that makes Egypt so unique. These hotels offer more than just a place to rest; they are an experience, often housed in buildings of historical significance or located in iconic neighborhoods that have shaped the city for centuries.

1.The Ritz-Carlton, Cairo
Location: Tahrir Square, Downtown Cairo
The Ritz-Carlton Cairo overlooks the Nile River and is situated right next to the Egyptian Museum, giving guests immediate access to some of the city's most celebrated landmarks. The hotel itself exudes elegance with its blend of European-style luxury and Egyptian influences. Marble floors, grand chandeliers, and exquisite artwork welcome

visitors into an environment that feels both opulent and inviting.

Guests can enjoy rooms with panoramic Nile views, dine in Michelin-star restaurants, or relax at the hotel's luxurious spa. Whether lounging by the pool or exploring nearby historical sites, this hotel provides the perfect balance of modern comfort and historical richness.

2. **Marriott Mena House, Cairo**

Location: Giza

Nestled at the base of the Giza Plateau, **Marriott Mena House** offers an incomparable view of the Great Pyramids, bringing the wonder of ancient Egypt right to your doorstep. The hotel itself is a historic landmark, having once hosted dignitaries, celebrities, and royalty since its opening in the 19th century.

The lush gardens, coupled with the grandeur of the hotel's interiors, make it an oasis of serenity, just a stone's throw away from one of the world's most iconic structures. Guests can dine al fresco with views of the pyramids, or unwind in lavish suites that combine traditional Egyptian decor with modern amenities.

3.**Four Seasons Hotel Cairo at Nile Plaza**

Location: Garden City, Cairo

Located in one of Cairo's most prestigious neighborhoods, **The Four Seasons Nile Plaza** offers a luxurious escape in the heart of the city. Overlooking the Nile, this hotel boasts spectacular views, especially at sunset when the river shimmers in the golden light. Its central location places guests within easy reach of the Egyptian Museum, the Cairo Opera House, and bustling Tahrir Square.

The hotel features elegantly designed rooms, top-notch dining options, and an indulgent spa. Whether lounging by the pool, taking a yoga class, or enjoying gourmet international cuisine, guests are treated to a high standard of luxury at every turn.

4.**Sofitel Cairo El Gezirah**
Location: Zamalek, Cairo
Perched on the southern tip of Zamalek Island in the Nile, **Sofitel Cairo El Gezirah** offers stunning 360-degree views of Cairo's skyline and the river. This French-inspired luxury hotel combines the elegance of Parisian flair with the cultural richness of Egypt. The circular design ensures that nearly every room and restaurant offers breathtaking vistas of the surrounding city and the Nile.

The hotel's unique location places it within walking distance of the Cairo Tower and the Cairo

Opera House. It also features an infinity pool that appears to spill directly into the Nile, adding an extra layer of charm to your stay. Whether enjoying a cocktail by the river or indulging in French-Egyptian fusion cuisine, Sofitel delivers a distinctly chic experience in the heart of Cairo.

5.Kempinski Nile Hotel Garden City Cairo
Location: Garden City, Cairo
Known for its boutique charm and intimate atmosphere, the **Kempinski Nile Hotel** in Garden City is a secret spot of luxurious refinement. Nestled on the banks of the Nile, the hotel offers an atmosphere of serenity, despite being in the center of the bustling city.

With spacious, stylishly appointed rooms and suites, many of which come with private balconies overlooking the river, guests are afforded a peaceful retreat. The hotel also offers a variety of fine dining options, including a rooftop restaurant with panoramic views of Cairo. Additionally, the spa offers personalized treatments that will leave you feeling completely rejuvenated after a day of exploration.

A Stay Steeped in History and Elegance
Luxury hotels in Cairo offer more than just high-end accommodations—they are a bridge

between the ancient and the contemporary. Each of these properties seamlessly integrates the timeless charm of Egypt's history with the comforts and conveniences of modern travel. Whether you're gazing at the pyramids from the lush gardens of Mena House or enjoying world-class cuisine overlooking the Nile, these hotels provide an experience that combines elegance, culture, and unmatched hospitality.

Each stay not only ensures comfort but offers an immersion into Cairo's rich history, with every corner of these hotels paying homage to the city's unique past. For travelers seeking a journey that weaves together history, luxury, and unforgettable moments, these hotels provide the perfect base for exploring Cairo's wonders.

Budget-Friendly Stays: Hostels and Guesthouses

While Cairo is famous for its luxury hotels and historic palaces, the city also offers a wide range of budget-friendly accommodations that cater to travelers seeking comfort and affordability. Hostels and guesthouses across the city are designed to give visitors a more intimate, local experience without compromising on essential comforts. Whether you're a solo traveler, a backpacker, or someone who simply prefers to save on accommodation to splurge elsewhere, these options ensure a memorable stay without stretching your budget.

1.Dahab Hostel
Location: Downtown Cairo
Tucked away on a quiet rooftop in the heart of the bustling downtown area, **Dahab Hostel** offers an oasis of calm in the midst of the city. Known for its relaxed, bohemian vibe, the hostel provides basic but comfortable accommodations, perfect for backpackers and budget travelers. The rooftop garden offers stunning views of the city, where guests can unwind after a day of exploring the chaotic streets of Cairo.

Dormitories and private rooms are available, and the staff is always on hand to help organize day trips to local attractions like the Pyramids of Giza or the Egyptian Museum. Prices for dorm beds start around **$10 USD** per night, while private rooms can range between **$20-30 USD**.

2.Meramees Hostel
Location Downtown Cairo
Conveniently located near Tahrir Square, **Meramees Hostel** is ideal for travelers who want to be within walking distance of Cairo's major

attractions, including the Egyptian Museum and the Nile River. The hostel boasts a warm, welcoming atmosphere, with staff that go out of their way to make guests feel at home.

Meramees offers both dorm-style accommodations and private rooms, each clean and simply furnished. Breakfast is included, and the shared lounge area is a great place to meet fellow travelers. Dorm beds typically cost around **$12-15 USD** per night, while private rooms are available from **$25-35 USD** per night.

3.**Australian Hostel**
Location: Downtown Cairo

A favorite among budget travelers, **Australian Hostel** is known for its excellent location and friendly service. Situated just a short walk from Tahrir Square, it's easy to access both the historical sites and vibrant streets of Cairo. The hostel offers free Wi-Fi, clean rooms, and helpful staff who are more than happy to assist in organizing tours around the city and beyond.

Guests can choose between shared dorms or private rooms, with dorm beds priced around **$10-15 USD** and private rooms ranging from **$25-40 USD**. The hostel also offers airport pickup services at a small additional fee, making it a convenient option for first-time visitors.

4. Pyramids View Inn
Location: Giza

For those looking to stay near one of Egypt's most iconic landmarks, **Pyramids View Inn** in Giza offers budget-friendly accommodations with a priceless view. This guesthouse is just a stone's throw away from the Pyramids of Giza, making it a fantastic option for travelers who want to wake up to the sight of the ancient wonders.

The rooms are basic yet comfortable, many of which feature terraces overlooking the pyramids. The rooftop offers breathtaking views, especially during the Sound and Light Show in the evening. Prices for rooms at Pyramids View Inn start from around **$30-50 USD** per night, including breakfast.

5. Arabesque Hotel
Location: Downtown Cairo

Located near Tahrir Square, **Arabesque Hotel** offers budget-friendly accommodations with an authentic Egyptian ambiance. The hotel's decor features traditional Arabesque designs, giving guests a more local feel during their stay.

The hotel is known for its helpful staff and convenient location, close to many cafes, restaurants, and the Egyptian Museum. Rooms are simple but comfortable, and the hotel offers free breakfast and Wi-Fi to all guests. Prices for private rooms range from **$20-40 USD** per night.

The Cairo Experience on a Budget
Staying in hostels or guesthouses while in Cairo doesn't mean sacrificing comfort or experience. These budget-friendly accommodations offer more than just a place to sleep—they provide a window into the local life of Cairo, a chance to connect with fellow travelers, and a home base that allows you to explore the city at your own pace. Many of these hostels and guesthouses are also centrally located, giving you easy access to Cairo's vibrant neighborhoods, historical landmarks, and bustling markets.

For those traveling on a budget, Cairo offers an array of accommodations that ensure your visit is both memorable and affordable. Whether it's the Pyramids just outside your window or the buzzing energy of downtown, these options will give you an authentic taste of Cairo without breaking the bank.

Boutique Hotels and Unique Lodging Experiences

For travelers seeking a more personalized and distinctive stay, Cairo's boutique hotels and unique lodging experiences offer a blend of style, history, and charm. Away from the grand international chains, these accommodations are known for their intimate settings, thoughtful design, and attention to detail. Whether you're staying in a restored historic mansion or a creatively designed modern space, these boutique hotels present a side of Cairo that is both unique and unforgettable.

1. Le Riad Hotel de Charme

Location: El Muizz Street, Islamic Cairo

Nestled in the heart of Cairo's historic district, **Le Riad Hotel de Charme** offers a boutique experience like no other. This 17-suite hotel is designed to reflect the opulence of traditional Arabian architecture, combined with modern comforts. Each suite is individually decorated, drawing inspiration from the rich history and culture of Cairo, and overlooks the vibrant streets of Old Cairo.

Staying at Le Riad feels like stepping back in time while enjoying contemporary amenities such as plush bedding, spacious rooms, and luxurious en-suite bathrooms. The hotel is surrounded by the historic charm of Islamic Cairo, with the vibrant Khan El Khalili market just steps away. Prices start at around **$200 USD** per night.

2.Villa Belle Époque
Location: Maadi

Tucked away in the leafy, upscale neighborhood of Maadi, **Villa Belle Époque** is a restored 1920s villa that provides a tranquil escape from the bustle of the city. The boutique hotel features individually designed rooms with period furnishings, lush gardens, and a serene pool area. The hotel prides itself on offering a personal and relaxed atmosphere, perfect for travelers who want to experience Cairo's quieter, residential side.

The property's restaurant serves freshly prepared meals with locally sourced ingredients, and the surrounding area of Maadi offers quaint cafes and dining spots. Prices for rooms at Villa Belle Époque start at **$180 USD** per night, making it an ideal retreat for those seeking luxury in a peaceful setting.

3.Talisman Hotel
Location: Downtown Cairo

For travelers who want to stay in the heart of the city without sacrificing charm,**Talisman Hotel** offers a cozy, boutique experience right in downtown Cairo. The hotel is housed in a 19th-century building and features intricately decorated rooms with antique furnishings, Persian carpets, and hand-painted ceilings, blending the old-world with the contemporary.

Talisman is known for its warm and personal service, with a small number of rooms that ensure a peaceful, private stay. The hotel's central location makes it easy to explore Cairo's top attractions, such as the Egyptian Museum, which is just a short walk away. Room rates start from **$150-170 USD** per night.

4. The Gabriel Hotel
Location: Heliopolis

A boutique hotel with a modern, elegant flair, **The Gabriel Hotel** is located in the upscale district of Heliopolis, close to Cairo International Airport. This luxurious boutique property offers a refined blend of French-inspired décor and contemporary design. Each room is decorated with a unique theme, featuring plush fabrics, crystal chandeliers, and marble bathrooms.

The hotel's restaurant, Salt, offers an exceptional fine-dining experience, with a menu blending Mediterranean and international cuisine. The Gabriel is ideal for travelers who want both convenience and luxury, with rooms starting at approximately **$140 USD** per night.

5.**Sofitel Cairo El Gezirah (Boutique Experience)**
Location: Zamalek
While **Sofitel Cairo El Gezirah** is part of an international brand, it offers a unique boutique experience within the context of Cairo's vibrant Zamalek district. Located on the southern tip of Gezira Island, the hotel combines modern luxury with panoramic views of the Nile. With its elegantly designed rooms, lush gardens, and luxurious amenities, it provides a more intimate and personal atmosphere than typical large hotels. The hotel's chic design incorporates elements of traditional Egyptian culture, blending them with modern aesthetics. Prices for rooms at Sofitel Cairo El Gezirah start from around **$180-220 USD** per night, and the hotel offers a range of dining options, including Nile-side restaurants.

A Blend of Style, History, and Local Flavor
Cairo's boutique hotels are not just places to rest—they are destinations in themselves, offering travelers a chance to experience the city's deep history and vibrant culture in a personal, intimate setting. Whether you prefer the leafy suburb of Maadi, the historic charm of Islamic

Cairo, or the modern luxury of Heliopolis, there's a unique lodging option for every type of traveler. Each of these accommodations captures the essence of Cairo in its own way, providing a truly unforgettable stay that will linger in your memory long after your journey ends.

Chapter Nine
Practical Information and Travel Tips

Best Times to Visit Cairo in 2025
When planning a trip to Cairo in 2025, timing is key to ensuring you get the most out of your experience. The city is vibrant and exciting year-round, but certain times of the year offer more comfortable weather, better events, and a more pleasant sightseeing experience.

Optimal Travel Seasons
-**Winter (November to February):** The winter months are considered the ideal time to visit Cairo. Temperatures range from 10°C (50°F) to 20°C (68°F), providing pleasant conditions for exploring the city's outdoor attractions, such as the Pyramids of Giza, Islamic Cairo, and the Nile's riverside walkways. Winter is also the season for fewer crowds, making it easier to enjoy popular sites without the bustling tourist throngs.
-**Spring (March to May):** Spring is another favorable time to visit, with slightly warmer temperatures between 15°C (59°F) and 25°C (77°F). The weather remains comfortable, and the landscape comes alive with blooming flowers and

greenery. Spring is also great for outdoor festivals and cultural events.

-**Autumn (September to October)**: Similar to spring, autumn offers moderate temperatures and a pleasant climate. While not as cool as winter, it's a good time for sightseeing and evening strolls along the Nile.

-**Summer (June to August)**: Cairo's summer is very hot, with temperatures often reaching 40°C (104°F). However, if you can handle the heat, this season can offer lower prices for accommodations and fewer tourists at major attractions.

Transportation: Getting Around the City

Navigating Cairo can be both exciting and challenging. The city's transportation system ranges from modern conveniences to more traditional means of travel, giving visitors various options depending on their preferences and budgets.

Public Transit

-**Cairo Metro**: One of the most efficient and cost-effective ways to get around Cairo is by using the metro system. It's particularly useful for traveling between central areas such as Downtown Cairo, Giza, and parts of Heliopolis. Tickets are very affordable, usually around **3-10 EGP**

($0.10-0.30 USD) depending on the number of stations.

-**Buses and Microbuses:** Cairo's extensive bus network covers most parts of the city. While cheap, buses can be crowded and a bit tricky to navigate for tourists unfamiliar with the routes. Microbuses, a more local form of shared transport, are quicker but often cramped.

-**Taxis**: Taxis are a common mode of transport, but it's recommended to use official, metered taxis or ride-hailing apps like **Uber** or **Careem**. They offer a more reliable service, and rides cost between **30-150 EGP** ($1-5 USD), depending on distance and traffic.

-**Ride-Sharing:** For those who prefer more comfort and less hassle, ride-hailing services like **Uber** and **Careem** are widely available and convenient. They are slightly more expensive than taxis but provide a safer and more predictable experience.

Traditional and Unique Transport

-**Feluccas**: For a scenic ride along the Nile, a traditional **felucca, the** boat offers a leisurely way to enjoy the river and its views. You can hire a felucca for a few hours, and prices range from **200-500 EGP** ($6-16 USD), depending on the duration.

-**Horse and Camel Rides**: Popular around the Pyramids of Giza, horse and camel rides provide a unique way to explore the desert landscape. Be prepared to negotiate prices, as rates can vary. A typical ride can cost around **150-400 EGP** ($5-13 USD).

Essential Arabic Phrases for Travelers

While many people in Cairo speak English, especially in tourist areas, learning a few key Arabic phrases will help you navigate the city and connect with locals on a deeper level. Here are some useful phrases to keep handy:

-**Hello**: مرحبا (Marhaba)
-**Goodbye**: مع السلامة (Ma'a as-salama)
-**Thank you**: شكراً (Shukran)
-**Please**: من فضلك (Min fadlak) for males / (Min fadlik) for females
-**Yes**: نعم (Na'am)
-**No**: لا (La)
-**How much is this?**: بكم هذا؟ (Bikam hatha?)
-**Excuse me**: عفواً (Afwan)
-**Where is the bathroom?**: أين الحمام؟ (Ayn al-hammam?)
-**Do you speak English?**: هل تتكلم الإنجليزية؟ (Hal tatakallam al-ingliziyya?)
-**Help!**: النجدة (An-najda)

Health, Safety, and Local Etiquette

Cairo is a relatively safe city for tourists, but there are some important health and safety tips to keep in mind while visiting.

Health
-**Stay Hydrated**: Cairo's climate, especially in the summer, can be extremely hot. Make sure to drink plenty of bottled water to stay hydrated.
-**Food Safety:** Street food is a delicious part of the Cairo experience, but it's important to be mindful of food hygiene. Stick to busy vendors where food turnover is high, and avoid raw or uncooked items.
-**Pharmacies**: Pharmacies are widespread in Cairo, and most of them carry over-the-counter medications. If you have specific health needs, it's wise to bring your own medication.

Safety
-**Petty Crime:** Like in any big city, petty crimes such as pickpocketing can occur, particularly in crowded areas like markets or public transport. Keep your valuables secure and be aware of your surroundings.
-**Tourist Scams**: Be cautious of overly friendly individuals offering unsolicited tours or services, especially near tourist attractions. Always verify

the credentials of guides or services before agreeing to anything.
-**Traffic Caution:** Cairo's traffic can be chaotic, so be careful when crossing streets. Pedestrian crossings are not always observed, and drivers may not stop for pedestrians.

Local Etiquette
-**Dress Modestly**: Cairo is a conservative city, especially outside of tourist areas. It's respectful to dress modestly, with women covering their shoulders and knees. Men should also avoid wearing shorts in certain areas.
-**Respect for Religious Sites:** When visiting mosques or religious places, dress appropriately. Women are typically required to cover their hair, and everyone should remove their shoes before entering.
-**Tipping (Baksheesh):** Tipping is a common practice in Egypt, often expected for small services such as hotel staff, drivers, or waiters. A tip of **5-10 EGP** ($0.20-0.30 USD) is customary for minor services, while **10-15%** of the bill is typical in restaurants.

Embrace the Journey
Visiting Cairo is an adventure in every sense, offering a blend of history, culture, and modern

city life. By choosing the right time to visit, mastering the city's transportation, picking up some basic Arabic phrases, and understanding local etiquette, you'll be well-prepared for a trip that is both immersive and unforgettable. Whether you're exploring the ancient wonders of Egypt or enjoying the modern hustle of downtown, Cairo in 2025 promises to be an experience like no other.

Chapter Ten
Sustainability and Responsible Tourism in Cairo

As travelers increasingly look for ways to reduce their environmental footprint, sustainability has become a key aspect of exploring a destination. Cairo, a city rich in both ancient heritage and modernity, is also making strides in promoting eco-conscious tourism. Travelers visiting Cairo in 2025 can experience the city's marvels while making responsible choices that benefit both the environment and the local community. Here's how to embrace sustainability while visiting Egypt's capital.

Eco-Friendly Accommodations

The hospitality industry in Cairo is evolving to meet the demands of eco-conscious travelers. Many hotels now focus on minimizing their environmental impact through various initiatives such as water conservation, energy efficiency, and the reduction of single-use plastics.

-**Steigenberger El Tahrir Hotel** (Tahrir Square): Located in the heart of Cairo, this hotel has made significant efforts in energy conservation and waste management. Steigenberger focuses on reducing water usage and uses eco-friendly products in their daily operations.

-**Marriott Mena House** (Pyramids Area): Overlooking the Pyramids of Giza, this luxury hotel not only offers stunning views but also incorporates sustainable practices like sourcing locally grown food, reducing energy consumption, and managing waste responsibly. Their approach to preserving the environment while maintaining a high level of comfort makes it a top choice for eco-conscious travelers.

-**Eco-Village in Fayoum Oasis** (near Cairo): A bit further from the bustling city, the Eco-Village offers a more rustic, sustainable experience for travelers who want to connect with nature. Using traditional building methods, the village is constructed from natural materials and operates with minimal impact on the environment. This is a great option for travelers seeking a getaway close to Cairo, while still focusing on sustainability.

-**Fairmont Nile City** (Corniche El Nile): Fairmont Nile City is committed to reducing its carbon footprint through energy-efficient measures, reducing waste, and participating in global environmental initiatives. Their "Green Partnership" program emphasizes recycling and supporting local sustainability efforts.

-**Le Méridien Pyramids Hotel & Spa**m (Giza): This iconic hotel, with views of the Pyramids, focuses on eco-friendly practices, such as efficient water usage and eco-conscious cleaning products. Le Méridien also works to reduce food waste through partnerships with local organizations.

Staying in eco-friendly accommodations allows travelers to enjoy Cairo's rich history and culture while knowing their stay contributes to a more sustainable future.

Sustainable Dining: Where to Eat Responsibly
Cairo's culinary scene is a fascinating blend of traditional Egyptian dishes and modern international cuisine. For travelers looking to dine sustainably, a few restaurants and eateries focus on sourcing local ingredients, reducing food waste, and promoting ethical food production.

-**Zooba** (Zamalek & Maadi): Zooba is a popular Egyptian street food restaurant that places a strong emphasis on sustainability. From using locally sourced ingredients to eliminating single-use plastics in packaging, Zooba showcases how fast food can be done in an eco-friendly way. The menu includes traditional dishes like koshari and taameya (Egyptian falafel), all prepared with fresh, responsibly sourced ingredients.

-**Osana Family Wellness Café** (Maadi): Located in Maadi, this café combines healthy, organic food with a strong focus on sustainability. They source their produce from local farms and support fair trade practices, making it a go-to spot for travelers looking for nutritious and environmentally responsible meals. Their menu features a range of vegan and vegetarian options.

-**Left Bank** (Zamalek): This chic Nile-side restaurant prioritizes sustainability by sourcing seasonal and organic produce for its dishes. Left Bank also supports local suppliers, which reduces its carbon footprint, while still offering a luxurious dining experience. The restaurant's menu features both international and Egyptian dishes.

-**Felfela** (Downtown Cairo): Felfela is a traditional Egyptian restaurant known for its commitment to sourcing fresh, local ingredients. Its menu includes classic Egyptian dishes, such as foul (fava beans), falafel, and grilled meats, all served in an environmentally conscious setting. Their focus on reducing waste and using sustainable ingredients makes it a responsible dining choice.

-**Naguib Mahfouz Café** (Khan El Khalili): While more of a cultural landmark than a restaurant, Naguib Mahfouz Café is famous for its support of local artisans and sustainable food sourcing. Located in the heart of Khan El Khalili, the café offers a sustainable approach to traditional Egyptian food, making it an ethical and authentic choice for visitors.

Opting for these restaurants not only provides a taste of Egyptian cuisine but also contributes to the sustainability of the local food industry, supporting both the environment and small-scale farmers.

Protecting Egypt's Historical Sites and Natural Environment

Cairo's vast array of historical monuments and archaeological sites, from the Pyramids of Giza to the ancient city of Memphis, are crucial not just to Egypt's heritage but to the history of human civilization. Preserving these wonders requires a collaborative effort from tourists, locals, and the government alike.

-**Respect Site Guidelines:** Whether you're visiting the Pyramids, the Sphinx, or the Egyptian Museum, it's essential to follow the guidelines set forth by Egypt's Ministry of Tourism and Antiquities. This includes avoiding climbing on monuments, not touching artifacts, and keeping areas clean of litter.

-**Conservation Initiatives:** Many historical sites in Egypt are part of conservation programs that aim to preserve the monuments for future generations. For example, the **Giza Plateau Conservation Program** focuses on protecting the pyramids from environmental damage caused by pollution, tourism, and natural erosion. As a traveler, it's important to support such initiatives by respecting barriers and avoiding activities that could damage the sites.

-**Sustainable Tour Operators:** Choose tour companies that have a commitment to responsible tourism practices. Many eco-friendly tour operators focus on minimizing their environmental impact by offering small group tours, offsetting carbon emissions, and supporting local conservation projects.

-Preserving Egypt's Natural Wonders: Beyond its monuments, Egypt's natural environment also requires protection. The Nile River, Egypt's lifeline, is a vital ecosystem that is vulnerable to pollution and overuse. When taking a Nile cruise, choose operators who emphasize eco-friendly practices, such as reducing plastic waste and minimizing fuel emissions. Also, avoid littering and use designated waste disposal areas.

-Support Local Communities: Responsible tourism also means contributing to the wellbeing of local communities. Consider visiting and supporting local artisans, cooperatives, and businesses in Cairo and surrounding areas. Purchasing locally made goods supports the livelihoods of families and promotes traditional crafts.

Embracing a Sustainable Future in Cairo

As a city that embodies thousands of years of history and culture, Cairo's future depends on both conservation and sustainable development. By choosing eco-friendly accommodations, dining responsibly, and respecting Egypt's priceless heritage, visitors in 2025 can play a part in preserving this remarkable city for future generations. Traveling sustainably in Cairo isn't just a trend, but a mindful way to appreciate the past while helping to shape a more eco-conscious future.

Chapter Eleven
Index

A

- **Al-Azhar Mosque and University**: A historic center of Islamic learning in Cairo.
- **Alexandria**: A coastal city offering a serene escape from Cairo, rich in history and Mediterranean charm.
- **Amr Ibn Al-As Mosque**: The first mosque built in Africa, located in Cairo's Fustat area.
- **Aswan**: A city in southern Egypt known for the Aswan High Dam, Philae Temple, and Nile River cruises.
- **Avenue of Sphinxes**: A monumental path in Luxor lined with hundreds of sphinx statues, connecting Karnak and Luxor Temples.

B

- **Bab Zuweila**: One of the gates of the old city of Cairo, offering panoramic views of Islamic Cairo.
- **Bayt Al-Suhaymi**: A traditional Ottoman-era house in Islamic Cairo, now a museum showcasing domestic life during the Ottoman period.

C

-**Cairo Citadel (Citadel of Saladin)** : A historic fortress that has been the seat of power for Egypt's rulers for centuries.

-**Cairo Opera House:** The main performing arts venue in Egypt, offering cultural experiences like ballet, opera, and concerts.

-**Coptic Cairo** : The Christian quarter in Cairo, home to historic churches, including the Hanging Church and the Coptic Museum.

D

- **Dahshur** : A lesser-visited archaeological site featuring the Bent Pyramid and Red Pyramid.
- **Downtown Cairo** : A vibrant area known for its modern architecture, bustling streets, and cultural landmarks like Tahrir Square.

E

-**Egyptian Museum** : A world-famous museum housing one of the largest collections of ancient Egyptian antiquities, including the treasures of King Tutankhamun.

- El Moez Street : A historic street in Islamic Cairo, lined with mosques, madrassas, and ancient buildings.

F

- **Fayoum Oasis** : A natural oasis located southwest of Cairo, known for its tranquil lakes, wildlife, and historical sites.
- **Felucca** : A traditional wooden sailboat used for leisurely cruises along the Nile River.

G

- **Giza Pyramids** : The iconic pyramids of Khufu, Khafre, and Menkaure, along with the Sphinx, one of the Seven Wonders of the Ancient World.
- **Grand Egyptian Museum (GEM)** : A new, state-of-the-art museum near the Giza Pyramids, set to open in 2025, showcasing ancient Egyptian artifacts.

H

-Hanging Church : One of the oldest and most famous churches in Coptic Cairo, built atop the gates of a Roman fortress.

- **Hatshepsut's Temple** : A mortuary temple built for the female pharaoh Hatshepsut, located in Luxor.

I

- **Islamic Cairo** : A historic area of Cairo filled with mosques, madrasas, and Islamic art, including landmarks like the Sultan Hassan Mosque and Al-Rifa'i Mosque.

K

- **Khan El Khalili** : Cairo's most famous bazaar, known for its narrow streets filled with shops selling jewelry, spices, textiles, and souvenirs.
- **Kom Ombo** : A unique double temple near Aswan, dedicated to the gods Sobek and Horus.

L

- **Luxor** : A city in southern Egypt known for its ancient temples, tombs, and monuments, including the Valley of the Kings and the Temples of Karnak and Luxor.

M

- **Mena House** : A luxury hotel near the Pyramids of Giza, famous for its historical significance and views of the ancient landmarks.
- **Memphis** : The ancient capital of Egypt, home to the ruins of the Temple of Ptah and a massive statue of Ramses II.
- **Mount Sinai** : A sacred mountain in the Sinai Peninsula, where Moses is said to have received the Ten Commandments.

N

-**Nile River**: The longest river in the world, running through Egypt and offering opportunities for cruises, felucca rides, and riverside dining.

P

-Philae Temple: An ancient temple complex dedicated to the goddess Isis, located on an island near Aswan.

Q

-**Qasr El-Nil Bridge**: A historic bridge in Cairo that offers beautiful views of the Nile River and connects Tahrir Square to Gezira Island.

R

- **Ramses II Statue** : A colossal statue of Pharaoh Ramses II, located at the Grand Egyptian Museum.
- **Rooftop Bars** : Popular venues in Cairo offering views of the Nile River and city skyline, perfect for evening relaxation.

S

- **Saqqara** : A vast ancient burial ground, home to the Step Pyramid of Djoser, the earliest colossal stone structure in Egypt.
- **Siwa Oasis:** A remote desert oasis in the Western Desert, known for its natural springs, olive groves, and historic ruins.

T

- **Temple of Karnak:** A massive temple complex in Luxor, dedicated to the Theban gods, particularly Amun-Ra.
- **Tahrir Square:** A major public square in downtown Cairo, known for its historical and political significance.

V

- **Valley of the Kings** : A royal burial site in Luxor, where tombs of pharaohs such as Tutankhamun and Ramses II are located.

W

-**Wadi El-Rayan:** A natural reserve near Fayoum, featuring waterfalls and diverse wildlife.

Z

-**Zamalek**: A leafy, upscale district on Gezira Island in Cairo, known for its embassies, cafes, and cultural venues like the Cairo Opera House.

CONCLUSION

As your journey through Cairo comes to an end, it's time to reflect on the extraordinary experiences that this vibrant city has offered. Cairo is not just a destination; it's a profound encounter with thousands of years of history, culture, and the human spirit. Whether you've wandered through the timeless relics of ancient Egypt, bargained for treasures in its bustling markets, or indulged in its rich culinary traditions, each moment in this city leaves a lasting imprint.

Cairo is a city where past and present coalesce in a unique way. It's a place where the awe-inspiring Pyramids of Giza, standing tall since the time of the Pharaohs, share the skyline with modern towers and new developments. Its contrasts are not jarring but rather a testament to how the city embraces both its ancient heritage and its future. Whether gazing at the architectural wonder of the Citadel, with its historical significance, or enjoying a contemporary rooftop bar overlooking the Nile, Cairo showcases a story of persistence, adaptation, and vibrancy.

The Timeless Appeal of Cairo's History

No trip to Cairo can be complete without reflecting on its monumental historical legacy. Standing before the Pyramids, the Sphinx, or exploring the treasures of the Egyptian Museum, it's impossible not to feel a deep connection to human history. The intricate carvings, the massive stone constructions, the delicate art forms preserved for millennia—these are not just relics but a living reminder of the ingenuity and spirit of an ancient civilization that continues to captivate the world.

Visiting the sprawling Saqqara necropolis or the temples of Luxor further deepens this understanding. It's not just the physical beauty of these sites but the cultural and spiritual significance they hold. For many travelers, exploring these monuments serves as a pilgrimage into the very origins of civilization.

Immersing Yourself in Cairo's Modern Culture

Beyond the history, Cairo offers a dynamic and colorful modern life. The streets are filled with energy—whether it's the lively markets of Khan El Khalili, where traders have peddled their wares for centuries, or the artistic and contemporary spirit you find in neighborhoods like Zamalek and Downtown Cairo. The city invites you to experience its layers, whether through its coffeehouses, art galleries, or performances of traditional music and dance.

Cairo is a place that rewards curiosity. Perhaps you wandered through the narrow alleyways of Islamic Cairo, discovering centuries-old mosques and madrassas or took a leisurely stroll along the Corniche, watching feluccas drift peacefully on the Nile. Maybe you spent your evenings in a cozy café, savoring local cuisine and engaging in friendly conversation with locals who are always eager to share their stories and traditions.

Discovering the People of Cairo

It's often said that the heart of Cairo lies in its people, and that's never more evident than when you engage with its residents. The warmth and hospitality you experience in Cairo are unforgettable, whether in the casual friendliness of a shopkeeper, the welcoming smile of a café owner, or a passerby helping you find your way through the city's labyrinthine streets. Egyptians take great pride in their city and are often eager to share their knowledge, offer recommendations, and ensure that your stay is enjoyable.

Cairo's Growing Future

As you look back on your time in Cairo, it's also worth noting how the city is evolving. The landscape is transforming with new developments, eco-friendly initiatives, and a growing focus on sustainability. From the ambitious Grand Egyptian Museum (GEM) set to house thousands of priceless artifacts to the green urban planning in New Cairo and the ongoing efforts to preserve Egypt's natural beauty, the city is not just preserving its past but also building a sustainable future.

Cairo is not merely a place to visit but a city that stays with you. It offers a unique combination of historical grandeur and modern life, where every street and every corner has a story to tell. Whether you've stayed for a few days or weeks, the memories of this city—the sounds of its streets, the breathtaking views of the Nile, the taste of its street food, and the profound experiences in its ancient landmarks—will remain with you long after you leave.

A Final Word on Traveling in Cairo

As your journey through Cairo concludes, it's important to remember that Cairo is a city of endless discovery. No matter how much time you spend here, there will always be more to explore. Whether you're drawn to its history, its culture, or its vibrant energy, Cairo has a way of inviting you back. Travelers leave with a sense of having experienced something much larger than themselves—a place where time, culture, and tradition blend seamlessly into one extraordinary experience.

As you prepare to depart, take with you the rich impressions of Cairo—a city where ancient wonders coexist with the modern world, where the Nile River continues to flow, carrying with it the stories of a civilization that has shaped human history. Whether you're planning a return trip or sharing your experiences with friends and family, Cairo will forever hold a special place in your memories, offering new layers of exploration with each visit.

Printed in Dunstable, United Kingdom